Love

AT FIRST THOUGHT?

Is your relationship a true meeting of like minds? In 1981, neurosurgeon Roger Sperry won the Nobel Prize for his definitive proof of the split-brain theory—which says that our physical, mental, and personality traits are all influenced by our brain bias. To discover which side of your brain is dominant—the left or the right—ask yourself:

- Do you prefer to print, or to write in script?
- Are you skilled at handling money, including balancing a checkbook?
- Do you prefer to relax by watching TV and listening to music, or by doing crossword puzzles and playing card games?
- When talking on the phone, are you more apt to doodle, or to make out a grocery list?
- Do you daydream a lot, or are you always involved in a more practical activity?
- Which of the following leisure activities do you enjoy?

hiking	swimming	tennis	bicycling
golf	walking	gardening	fishing
reading	camping	writing	drawing

To score your answers—and find out more about what brain dominance means in your love life—see Chapter 1. It's just one of the many fascinating aspects of your total compatibility profile!

Perfect
PARTNERS:

THE COUPLES' COMPATIBILITY GUIDE

Perfect PARTNERS

The Couples' Compatibility Guide

E L L E N   L E D E R M A N

POCKET BOOKS

New York   London   Toronto   Sydney   Tokyo   Singapore

An *Original* publication of POCKET BOOKS

POCKET BOOKS, a division of Simon & Schuster Inc.
1230 Avenue of the Americas, New York, NY 10020

Lederman, Ellen, 1954–
    Perfect partners : the couple's compatibility guide / Ellen
Lederman.
        p.   cm.
    ISBN 0-671-70262-9 : $8.95
    1. Married people—Psychology. 2. Interpersonal relations.
3. Marriage compatibility tests. I. Title.
HQ734.L3756   1990
646.7′7—dc20   90-34735
                                                CIP

First Pocket Books trade paperback printing July 1990

10 9 8 7 6 5 4 3 2 1

POCKET and colophon are registered trademarks of
Simon & Schuster Inc.

Printed in the U.S.A.

CONTENTS

INTRODUCTION

Who is your ideal mate? Hopefully, you've already found him or her. But whether you are currently in a long-term relationship or just getting to know someone, *Perfect Partners* will help you understand more about you and your partner's compatibility.

Psychologists, metaphysicians, and New Age practitioners have developed a variety of systems that give insights into individual personality traits. There are many books available that provide in-depth exposure to such methods of self-discovery as astrology, numerology, and palmistry. But information about other personality theories involving eye color, birth order research, color analysis, or blood type is not as readily available to the general public. Furthermore, most of the resources available focus on self-knowledge and don't discuss the compatibility of one type versus another.

Perfect Partners is the first comprehensive guide to understanding the kind of relationship you're likely to have with your mate. Fifteen different tests that you can take with (or for) your partner help you determine your rightness for each other.

Each section in the book includes a quiz or exercise that you and your partner can take together or separately. After you score your results, read the detailed analysis of the compatibility of your particular combination that follows. While each section can stand on its own, yielding an individualized relationship profile based on the system used in that section, the book also provides an overall total compatibility score. It is strongly recommended that while you consider the information in each individual section, you place greater emphasis on the total compatibility score, since this reveals the general trends of your entire relationship. Some sections are limited in scope because they address only one particular area (e.g., brain dominance focuses on thinking styles whereas heart lines on a hand deal with the more emotional and romantic aspects of personality). All have been tested by science or experience, but many are not in-depth enough to be foolproof on their own. As a group, however, the tests should serve as reliable guides to compatibility; hence, I strongly recommend you refer to your total compatibility score based on the sum of your scores in *all* the sections.

Obtaining your total compatibility score is extremely simple. Just tear out one of the score sheets you'll find at the back of the book. After reading each profile, note and record the accompanying score. You should record a score for every section you work on. (Note that for the section on hands, there are actually three different scores that you need to record—one each for the life, head, and heart line. Record all these scores, add them together, and then divide by three to get your overall hand score).

If, in some sections, one pairing alone does not suffice (i.e., you and your partner are both a red-blue pair as well as a red-green pair because you couldn't decide whether blue or green is your favorite color), you should use whichever profile is most accurate after reading all applicable ones. Thus, if the red-blue profile seems more representative of your relationship than the red-green one, choose the red-blue score for the section on color preference.

You may notice that when you choose a couple of different options and therefore arrive at more than one compatibility profile, some of the information is contradictory. For example, if you like both running and swimming in the exercise preference section, you may find that your profile for swimming-martial arts is much more positive than a second profile may be for running-martial arts. Don't let this concern you. Relationships are complex and ever-changing. One of your choices may reveal one thing about your relationship, whereas another choice addresses another aspect of the dynamics of your relationship which may be present at times. Consider all the relevant profiles for the varied information they can offer.

The fifteen different sections in the book are weighted according to their scientific validity and relevance to love relationships. Scores range (from low to high) as follows:

1 to 12
Brain dominance

1 to 10
Birth order
Handwriting

1 to 6
Humor appreciation
Color preference
Sleep position
Exercise preference
Pets
Decorating style
Food preference
Birth experience

1 to 5
Body type
Eye color
Hand type
Blood type

You'll find your specific score for each section adjacent to the profile you select. After recording and adding up your scores on the total compatibility score sheet, turn to the Total Compatibility Profiles at the end of the book to find your total compatibility profile.

Ideally, the two of you should work together on the quizzes and in reading your compatibility profiles. It's a fun way of getting to know each other (which is important whether you've been together two weeks or twenty years). But be honest in answering the quizzes; otherwise, the information in your designated profile will be invalid.

Obviously, you should not end a relationship on the basis of one (or even many) negative compatibility profile(s). There can be other variables in your relationship that have a bearing on your unique personalities and are not contained within the pages of this book. Remember, too, that this book is by no means a substitute for professional marriage counseling when serious problems exist.

But do use the information in *Perfect Partners* as a means of learning about the way the two of you interact. If you find that you have less going for you as a couple than you would like or that you have the potential for a negative relationship, don't consider this a negative reflection on either of you. There is no best type of person; there are simply some types who do well together naturally and others who need to work a little harder at getting along. Both kinds of relationships can benefit from the enhanced mutual understanding I hope the book will bring you.

May you always be blessed with the kind of love that's right for you.

ELLEN LEDERMAN

Brain Dominance

In 1981, neurosurgeon Roger Sperry won the Nobel Prize for his definitive proof of the split-brain theory. According to this theory, our physical and mental abilities as well as our personality traits are influenced by our brain bias (tendency to use one side of the brain more than the other) which results in a distinct brain-style (i.e., analytical and verbal vs. intuitive and visual).

Normally the hemispheres do not function independently. The two halves communicate through the connecting structure known as the corpus callosum. But in most people, there is a definite preference for one side of the brain. The simplest method for pinpointing this preference is to look at your handedness. If you're right-handed, you're most likely left-brain dominant. If you're among the twenty percent of the population who uses their left hands, chances are you're right-brained. But many people are ambidextrous to varying degrees. They may use their right hand for some tasks and the left hand for others. The discovery of your brain dominance can be further complicated by other factors such as the eye, ear, and foot you favor.

To determine whether you're predominantly left- or right-sided, take the following quiz. Look at where the majority of answers fall for each of you. Your brain dominance is the opposite of your sidedness. For example, if you seem to be right-sided, you have left-

1

brain dominance. If your answers are distributed evenly between the right side *and* left side (typical more of females than males), you probably possess characteristics of both right-brain and left-brain dominance. Compare your brain dominances and read on to learn about your compatibility.

Quiz

Circle the appropriate response to each question. If you find it difficult to answer some of the questions because you sometimes prefer your right side and at other times choose your left, try to keep the following guideline in mind: Designate which hand, foot, ear, eye, or side of your mouth you would use if you were allowed to use only this side for the rest of your life and were not allowed to use the other.

1. Which hand do you use to write with?
2. Which hand do you use to scratch your back?
3. Hold a pencil in your right hand and draw a circle. Note the direction your draw it (clockwise or counterclockwise). Now draw a circle with your left hand. If you drew both circles in a counterclockwise direction, circle "right." If you drew either or both circles in a clockwise direction, circle "left."
4. On which side of your mouth do you chew food?
5. Which foot do you tap to music?
6. Sit in a relaxed position and clasp your hands loosely together in your lap. Which thumb is on top?
7. Clap your hands. Which hand is on top?
8. Wink. Which eye does the winking?
9. When you use the telephone, which ear do you hold the receiver to?
10. Fold your arms in front of you. Which one is in front of the other?
11. Draw a profile of a dog. If you drew the profile facing to the left, circle "right." If you drew it facing to the right, circle "left."
12. If you kicked a ball, which foot would you use?
13. If you were allowed to either print or write in longhand anytime you needed to write a letter (and were not permitted to combine the two), would you prefer printing (circle "left") or writing in longhand (circle "right")?

Person 1		Question	Person 2	
R	L	1	R	L
R	L	2	R	L
R	L	3	R	L
R	L	4	R	L
R	L	5	R	L
R	L	6	R	L
R	L	7	R	L
R	L	8	R	L
R	L	9	R	L
R	L	10	R	L
R	L	11	R	L
R	L	12	R	L
R	L	13	R	L

NOTE: Brain dominance is contralateral to your sidedness. If you're left-sided, you have right-brain dominance; right-sidedness indicates left-brain dominance. Since both the quiz above and the alternative below have an odd number of questions, you will end up with more points on either the right or left sides. However, the two quizzes together might not give you a clear majority on one of the sides. For instance, you might score eight on one of the sides for the quiz above or six for the same side with the quiz below. This would indicate a mixed brain dominance in which both sides of the brain play a role. In such a case, you should score your brain dominance on page 7 by writing a 1 in the blank next to the brain dominance where most of your answers fall and a 2 for the other side. Your partner should also do the same if the two quizzes do not indicate a clear brain dominance in his or her case either. You'll want to take special note of the profile for your primary combination (i.e., if your 1 fell under left and your partner's 1 fell under right, you'd need to consult the R-L profile). But you also want to read the profile for your secondary combination (i.e., if you recorded a 2 under right, you'd want to look up the R-R profile) since this can reveal some aspects of your pairing which may surface from time to time.

Alternative Quiz

If your partner is not available to take the preceding quiz, you can answer the following questions on your own to determine whether she or he is right- or left-brained. As with the preceding quiz, you may find that both options of certain questions seem true at different times. For example, your partner may sometimes prefer to relax by watching TV or listening to music, but at other times would choose to do crossword puzzles or play card games. For the purposes of this quiz, try to determine which your partner would choose if forced to decide between the two options and would have to permanently adhere to this decision. Ask yourself: If my partner could do or be only one of these choices, which one would she or he choose?

1. Does she or he prefer to print (R) or write in script (L)?
2. Is she or he skilled at handling money, including balancing the checkbook?
   If yes, L
   If no, R
3. Does she or he express thoughts and feelings better with words (L) or actions(R)?
4. Would she or he prefer to relax by:
   watching TV or listening to music? (R)
   doing crossword puzzles or playing card games? (L)
5. When talking on the phone, is she or he apt to doodle (R) or make out the grocery list (L)?
6. Is she or he right-handed (L) or left-handed (R)?
7. Does she or he have a taste for the unusual (R) or prefer what's familiar (L)?
8. Does she or he tend to daydream a lot (R) or is always involved in a more practical activity (L)?
9. Which of the following groups of leisure activities does she or he most enjoy? (Choose either the ones marked R or the ones marked L.)

hiking-L	swimming-R	tennis-L	bicycling-R
golf-L	walking-R	gardening-L	fishing-R
reading-L	camping-R	writing-L	drawing-R

Person 1	Question	Person 2
R L	1	R L
R L	2	R L
R L	3	R L
R L	4	R L
R L	5	R L
R L	6	R L
R L	7	R L
R L	8	R L
R L	9	R L

See the note after the first quiz if you find that your answers don't fall in a clear majority (i.e., at least six under either right or left). Remember that unlike the first quiz, which determines sidedness and which has to be reversed to determine brain dominance, the alternative quiz measures actual brain dominance. If most of your answers on the alternative quiz fall under R, you may then consider yourself to be right-brained.

Person 1	Brain Dominance	Person 1
_____	Right	_____
_____	Left	_____

	RIGHT RIGHT	10

Life is never dull when both partners are right-brained! Both of you are as playful and spontaneous as a child. If there's something you want to do, you do it—without any thought beforehand or guilt afterward. This mutual trait ensures that your relationship will remain lively, but it is also responsible for impulsive actions that can have negative consequences. Spur-of-the-moment purchases of small items or decisions to go away for the weekend are one thing, but indulging other whims without considering the ramifications can be disastrous. A dual right-brained couple is very likely to experience financial difficulties or episodes of infidelity because one or both partners didn't curb their impulses and acted rashly.

You're a talented couple. Each of you undoubtedly excels in one or more of the visual or performing arts or in sports. You do need to avoid becoming too competitive with each other since that can wreak havoc on any relationship. Fortunately, you both are blessed with your own creative or motor talents and shouldn't feel insecure about your respective partner's gifts. And neither of you is overly concerned about fame or fortune. When you paint, draw, sculpt, dance, act, run, perform gymnastics, or participate in athletics, you do it for enjoyment's sake. It's an outlet for expressing your individuality, not a business venture for acquiring wealth or earning recognition.

Right-brained individuals are not good at expressing themselves in words. Neither of you is gifted verbally. You both find it difficult to talk about your feelings and needs. This usually isn't a major problem since you're each able to communicate in nonverbal ways. Whereas left-brained couples are limited to verbal methods of declaring love or rendering an apology, you can use more creative means such as finding just the right gift, drawing a picture, or doing something special for your partner that says "I love you" or "I'm sorry" more eloquently than words ever could.

| **RIGHT** | **LEFT** | 12 |

A right-brained/left-brained couple is a study in contrasts. The right-brained partner is impulsive, whereas the left-brained one is a planner. The right-brained individual is intuitive and visual; the left-brained person is analytical and verbal. The left-brained partner's serious nature is the opposite of the right-brained partner's childlike spontaneity. The left-brained partner tends to be neat; the right-brained individual can be sloppy. The right-brained partner enjoys variety and change whereas the left-brained partner is most comfortable with a rigid order and stability.

Your differences will often cause misunderstandings and arguments. The left-brained partner will never understand why the right-brained partner can't balance a checkbook. The right-brained partner will be exasperated by his or her left-brained counterpart's insistence on carefully considering the consequences prior to taking any action. Words come easily to a left-brained person, but the left-brained individual lacks this verbal facility and is apt to be vague or inappropriate when attempting to put his or her thoughts and feelings into words. This can be frustrating to the more eloquent left-brained partner. Still another contrast is that of the right-brained mood swings with the left-brained partner's relatively stable emotions. And even your leisure interests will be diametrically opposed. The left-brained partner enjoys competitive activities such as golf, tennis, or bridge, and verbal pursuits such as reading and writing; the right-brained partner prefers outdoor activities such as swimming, camping, hiking, fishing, or even just doing nothing but relaxing.

A right-brained/left-brained relationship can work beautifully or it can fizzle within a short period of time. The two of you control your relationship's destiny. You can resent your partners for not being more like yourselves and you can even try to change him or her, but this strategy is not recommended. It is far preferable to learn to accept your differences and to perceive your partner's qualities as being highly desirable since they perfectly complement your own.

LEFT	LEFT		8

The two of you are apt to have a relationship that is run like a business. As much as possible, you try to prevent unproductive emotions from interfering in your lives. Right-brained couples may act on their gut feelings, but not you. You're both careful to keep things sensible, organized, and on schedule. Efficiency is something you both strive for. Since it can be costly in terms of time and energy to deal with certain feelings as they arise, you tend to ignore them and focus instead on the day-to-day material necessities of your lives. What you don't realize is that this practice can be costly in terms of your happiness and cohesiveness as a couple. If you don't make the effort to fully communicate with each other, your relationship will never grow and might even deteriorate.

Verbalizing your thoughts is not a problem for either of you. Left-brained individuals are very proficient in oral self-expression. When you finally get around to making time in your busy schedules to talk over your problems, you don't have to hunt for ways to say whatever's on your mind(s). But you share a tendency to expound too much, often talking things to death. You're apt to analyze your emotions rather than feeling them. This prevents you from experiencing the knock-down, drag-out fights known to other couples, but it also causes your relationship to be somewhat mechanistic and superficial.

Spontaneity is not often present in your lives. You'd rather plan everything out so you act in the rational, organized style that is characteristic of the left-brained. This is considered an asset in the business world, but it does little to enhance your relationship. Your life together can easily become too predictable and dull. To keep the romance alive, try to arrange for little surprises (e.g., unplanned picnics) just for the fun of it.

2

Birth Order

Your parents and siblings may not play a large role in your current life, but they had a great deal of influence in shaping your personality as you were growing up. The position in which you were born within the framework of your family affects the way you cope with people and the world at large even today. As the oldest, middle, youngest, or only child in your family, you were probably treated a certain way that is unique to that birth position. For example, a firstborn child tends to be closer to his or her parents and to be disciplined more strictly than later children. The firstborn therefore has a tendency to develop certain characteristics such as being more conscientious, achievement-driven, and rigid in his or her ways than a middle or youngest child. Thus these birth order personality traits will affect how you and your partner relate to each other in adult life.

All you need to do to find out whether the two of you are compatible is to pair your individual birth orders and then read the appropriate profile. Note that in some circumstances your actual birth order may not accurately reflect the experiences you had as a child. For example, a youngest child born many years after his or her older siblings may be raised similarly to an only child (particularly if the siblings leave the house while the youngest is growing up). Similarly, a firstborn child may experience many years of being an only child until a brother or sister comes along.

9

While you and your family are really the only ones who can determine what birth order you experienced if the situation wasn't clear-cut, use the following guidelines to help you choose.

Oldest child by more than eighteen years
   Consider yourself an only child.
Oldest child by more than seven years but less than eighteen
   You have almost as many "only" characteristics as "oldest." Put a check on both these lines.
Youngest child by more than eighteen years
   Consider yourself an only.
Twins
   Interestingly, twins are considered to have a birth order even if only by minutes or hours. If your twin is the only sibling you have, one of you can be considered the youngest and the other the oldest. If you have older siblings and no younger ones, the oldest twin may be considered a middle while the younger twin is the youngest in the family. If you have both older and younger siblings, you can probably consider yourselves both to be middle children.

Person 1	Birth order	Person 2
_____	Only	_____
_____	Oldest	_____
_____	Middle	_____
_____	Youngest	_____

NOTE: If you checked off more than one birth order (*i.e.*, only and oldest), you will need to compare both these answers with those of your partner since you have characteristics of both birth orders. If, for example, your partner is a youngest, you'll need to read both the Only-Youngest and Oldest-Youngest profiles since there may be aspects of both dynamics in your relationship.

ONLY   ONLY   7

If both of you grew up without siblings, you probably are more self-confident than most people. Because you feel so secure with yourselves and your place in the world, you can have a relationship that is free of the petty jealousies and insecurities that other couples experience. You both are highly sophisticated and worldly, so you're able to achieve a life-style filled with trendy, interesting people and places. Each of you most likely has highly developed verbal abilities and is able to express your feelings and thoughts well. As a result, you're able to avoid the misunderstandings that result from a lack of communication.

But there can be some problems within a double-only child pairing. You both tend to be very self-indulgent, usually opting to do whatever pleases each of you at the moment instead of considering what would be best for you as a couple in the long run. There's a tendency to behave selfishly, without thinking of the other person. You also may find yourselves drifting apart unless you make a concerted effort to spend sufficient quality time together. Since you're both so self-sufficient and independent, there is a strong likelihood that you'll be so busy doing your own individual things that you'll neglect each other. This can be disastrous for a relationship, so be sure to stay fully involved in your partner's life.

ONLY   OLDEST   8

First, the good news about your pairing. The only child will respect the oldest child's self-control and discipline, especially since it enables the oldest to achieve so much in life. If the two of you can work through your (many) problems, you'll be able to accomplish all your mutual and individual goals.

Unfortunately, there will be many instances where you really don't understand each other. The oldest child prefers to take the traditional route whenever possible, whereas the only child feels secure enough to experiment with the new and unknown. The only child will have difficulty relating to the oldest's need for approval and for trying to be all things to all people. As far as the only child is concerned, attempting to please everyone else is futile; he or she feels the need only to be true to him- or herself. But the oldest child doesn't share this perspective and will knock him- or herself out trying to please. It's quite possible that the oldest will resent the only's independent nature and feel that the only doesn't care enough to try to make his or her partner happy. When at times the oldest becomes jealous or anxious, the self-assured only won't be able to relate to these emotions. However, the only child is very likely to have excellent verbal skills and will be able to express his or her feelings of love, thus reassuring the oldest and helping to calm what could otherwise be a stormy relationship.

ONLY	MIDDLE	9

The two of you should get along well for the most part. You're different in several ways, but your characteristics complement each other's. For example, the only child tends to be somewhat of a loner whereas the middle child is highly social. A close relationship with a middle child will help expand the only child's social network and prevent him or her from becoming too reclusive. The only child can enhance the middle's personal growth, showing him or her how to use introspection for self-knowledge and improvement. Another difference is your level of ambition. The only child has a drive to succeed whereas the middle child wants only to make life as pleasant as it could possibly be. While the only child may look askew at the middle's lack of ambition at times, she or he is usually astute enough to realize that the middle child has other attributes that are equally appealing. The middle child may not be committed to getting ahead in the world, but she or he has a warm interest in other people. In an only-middle pairing, the only child is the beneficiary of the middle's caring and concern.

The only potential problem area is that the only child has a great deal of emotional stability while the middle child experiences more fluctuations in mood and temperament. Because the only child is likely to have difficulty coping with the middle's ups and downs, the middle needs to try to avoid emotional extremes and function as consistently as possible.

ONLY	YOUNGEST		5

As an only child and youngest child, the two of you are as different from each other as night and day. The youngest child tends to be highly emotional whereas the only child is more self-contained and tends to verbalize his or her feelings rather than act them out. Dependency is another big issue between you. The youngest child's reliance on other people creates some difficulties for the only child, who fights his or her own need to be protected from the dangers and stresses of life. The only child is sometimes apt to resent having to take care of the youngest and will wish that just occasionally, she or he could be the one who is being looked after rather than always being the leader. You'll also be wary of each other's tactics for getting what you want. The self-confident only child automatically expects to be given whatever she or he wishes without even having to ask or negotiate. The youngest doesn't expect anything to be handed to him or her; he or she knows that it will be necessary for him or her to work hard and will resort to any means (even devious ones) to get what is desired. Obviously each of you will be uncomfortable with the other's approach to self-fulfillment.

But while an only-youngest pairing has its share of problems, it also has its up side. With the only child's sophistication and intellectual inclinations and the youngest child's creativity, the two of you can lead a very stimulating life together. There's no limit to the exciting challenges that you can create for yourselves.

OLDEST	OLDEST		6

Because the two of you are so much alike, your being together can accentuate your mutual positive characteristics but it can also bring out your worst sides. The best-case scenario is that because you each expect so much of yourselves, you'll both put forth maximum effort to be a wonderful partner in every way possible. Your mutual dependability enables your respective partners to always be able to count on you. Since you're both conscientious and competitive, you'll work hard to ensure that you achieve everything you want as a couple. Your independent natures give each other room to grow as individuals.

But these same traits are just as likely to cause difficulties in your relationship. The high expectations and standards that you set for yourselves can lead to dissatisfaction when they're not attained. If you're not feeling good about yourselves, you won't feel good about each other and your relationship. Your competitiveness can also be a problem. Both of you share a tendency to become jealous when someone else succeeds to a greater extent than you. Rather than being supportive of each other, you may actually put barriers in the other person's way. Still another concern is your shared conformity. As long as you're together, you'll avoid trying anything new or different. It's very likely that you'll dig yourselves deep into a rut. But, as two oldest children, you have the discipline and drive to accomplish whatever you want. If you want your relationship to endure and prosper, you both have the ability to make it happen.

OLDEST   MIDDLE   **10**

You'll have a happy relationship, thanks in large part to the easygoing middle child. Although you're very different from each other, you're able to function as equal partners in the relationship. Because the middle has learned how to effectively deal with all types of people, she or he is a good negotiator and can prevent the oldest from becoming too dictatorial. The oldest may not enjoy compromising at first, but the middle will be able to convince him or her of the benefits of doing so.

You complement each other in many ways. The oldest child is very ambitious whereas the middle is much more concerned with human relations. Therefore, the oldest is mostly task-oriented, working hard to achieve specific, concrete goals while the middle is people-oriented, more interested in enjoying the social aspects of his or her life. The middle child conforms strongly to peer values; the oldest is more independent and self-motivated. But these differences work in your favor. Your respective partners make both of you more complete as individuals. Other people may want a partner who is just like them, but an oldest-middle pairing is as compatible (if not more so) than couplings of the same birth order.

| OLDEST   YOUNGEST | 1 |

Because the two of you have such entirely different perspectives, you'll have to put forth considerable effort to find some common ground. One of the major dissimilarities in your temperaments is that the youngest is playful and lighthearted while the oldest tends to be tense, serious, and driven. The oldest is very conservative whereas the youngest doesn't like to conform to tradition. A strong sense of spirituality and a high degree of creativity are usually found in youngest children, but this is far from the case with the oldest. The oldest child's feet are firmly planted in the material world; she or he is too busy dealing with the demands of everyday life to be concerned with finding beauty and meaning in the world at large.

The differences between you will always remain, but you can learn to be empathetic to each other's concerns rather than constantly questioning and criticizing every move your partner makes. Accept each other for who you are without expecting perfect compatibility. When the youngest feels the need for frequent socializing and large group affairs, she or he should generally pursue these activities alone since the oldest prefers to have a few close friendships and doesn't enjoy the same type of social involvement the youngest thrives on. Be cognizant of the potential for power struggles in your relationship. When the youngest child occasionally wants the same power and control in the relationship, the oldest child has difficulty giving in gracefully since she or he wants the upper hand and tends not to view the youngest as a true equal. If you both are willing to discuss your needs and concerns honestly and to resolve them fairly, you'll get along much better.

| MIDDLE   MIDDLE | 7 |

There's a lot of positive things to be said about a relationship involving two middle children. You both have excellent interpersonal skills and, because you understand what makes other people tick and how to handle them, you deal with each other in a highly effective manner. Other partners might have trouble dealing with the fluctuating temperament of a middle child, but one middle child can empathize with the mood swings of another. Chances are you won't experience many problems together, but when you occasionally do, your mutual ability to compromise will always keep your relationship on steady ground. Neither of you is competitive by nature, so you'll do everything you can to support each other.

The only negative aspect is that neither partner grows in a dual-middle relationship. You can become so involved with each other that you lose track of all your other friends. Since neither of you is terribly ambitious, you won't encourage the other to dream big and to strive to achieve his or her goals. You'll bring out the conformist in each other and will avoid experimenting with anything that's the least bit innovative or different. There's no doubt you'll be extremely comfortable in this relationship, but it may compromise your individuality and potential for growth.

MIDDLE   YOUNGEST   **8**

A middle-youngest pairing can be successful but it does have a pitfall you need to watch out for. Although the middle child can be very tolerant, she or he may still come to resent the youngest's dependence. The middle child may not be a superachiever in any aspect of his or her life, but is more autonomous than the youngest child. A serious rift can occur if it ever gets to the point where the middle feels taken advantage of by the youngest. Obviously, the way to avoid this is for the youngest to learn to become more self-reliant and make less demands on his or her partner.

Aside from this problem, the two of you should be happy together. You may not achieve much in the way of material riches, but you'll enjoy a full social life and find lots of laughter with each other. The youngest child's lighthearted nature and sense of humor enables him or her to cope with the middle's emotional peaks and valleys. Even when the middle child is in a foul mood, the youngest can find a way to make you both smile. The youngest child may help the middle discover his or her own individuality instead of blindly conforming to what's expected or traditional. And while the youngest child can sometimes be less than forthright and honest in attempting to get what she or he wants, the middle child has an excellent grasp of human nature and can tolerate occasions where the youngest behaves in devious ways.

YOUNGEST YOUNGEST	6

You can be an ideal couple . . . but you're just as likely to be the worst possible choice for each other. Your compatibility depends on how you were treated as the youngest child in both your families. If your older siblings treated you with respect and affection, you'll be able to treat your respective partners with kindness and sensitivity. But if you were teased, laughed at, or taken advantage of, you may find it difficult to fully trust someone else. If this is the case, you may not relate to each other in a positive way. You may resort to cutting each other down in underhanded ways in an attempt to try to have some control and power. Each of you may do destructive things to the other in an attempt to avoid getting hurt first.

But as mentioned earlier, a double-youngest coupling can be gentle and supportive. You can bring out the best in each other. Together you can achieve new heights of creativity and spirituality, fully becoming the persons you were meant to be. Even as adults you don't lose your playful natures. This adds a lot of joy to your life together. You know how to let loose and have fun. Everyday stresses don't bother you as much as they do other couples, so you'll have more energy to devote to your relationship. If you try hard to keep things on the right track, you'll have something very special indeed.

3

Handwriting

Although handwriting analysis has been practiced for many years, graphology is just now beginning to gain scientific acceptance. People are recognizing that handwriting does reflect the personality characteristics of the writer and are even using it for such purposes as employment decisions (who to hire, who to promote).

There are many aspects of handwriting that can be analyzed (e.g., slant, pressure, size, dotting of *i*'s). But signatures can be considered our true trademarks, revealing how we see ourselves and how we'd like the world to view us.

To analyze whether your signatures indicate a basic compatibility or not, simply find something (e.g., a letter or check) that you've signed and determine which type each of your signatures falls under. Then combine your answers to find the profile that describes you as a couple.

TYPE A

No real left or right slant; no embellishments such as underlining; easy to read.

John Doe

TYPE B

Embellished with large capitals, flourishes, etc., or underscored with a wavy line.

Sue Coleman

Carole Johnson

TYPE C

Underscored with a straight or zigzagged line, or underscored with the ending stroke.

Andrew Jefferson

TYPE D
Final stroke curled back over name or encircling name, or indistinct signature.

TYPE E
Slanted to the left.

TYPE F
Slanted to the right.

Karen Evens

TYPE G
Slanted upward.

Betsy Webb

TYPE H
Slanted downward.

David Jones

TYPE I
Starts out being legible but dissolves into a snakelike indistinct scribble.

Chris Robertson

Person 1	Type	Person 2
_____	A	_____
_____	B	_____
_____	C	_____
_____	D	_____
_____	E	_____
_____	F	_____
_____	G	_____
_____	H	_____
_____	I	_____

A   A   **10**

You'll do well together because you always relate to each other in an honest, straightforward way. No pretenses or games in your relationship; you each are who you are and you're both comfortable with your identities. Because you're at peace with your individual selves, you're well able to accept and support your respective partners.

A   B   **10**

This is a great relationship! You'll have a wide circle of friends whom you enjoy, but you'll also find much pleasure in spending time together by yourselves. The A partner will appreciate the spark that the B's creativity brings to his or her life. The B will feel more secure with the down-to-earth A, knowing that the A can be counted on to be a supportive, understanding partner, even when the B doesn't use good judgment in what she or he says or does.

A   C   9

Yours is a dynamic pairing. The C tends to want to assume a leadership role, but the A usually won't mind allowing his or her partner to call most of the shots. Together you'll feel free to explore the world and discover all it offers. Because you both enjoy such good mental health, you'll have a relationship filled with laughter and love.

A   D   3

The D will feel better with a stable, easygoing partner like the A, but the feeling isn't reciprocated. Although the A will try hard to cope with the D's insecurities, there will be times when the A will be ready to give up on the relationship. The D requires constant reassurance and encouragement and the A finds this draining. The prognosis for your relationship is not good unless the D can learn to allay some of his or her self-doubts and fears about the world at large.

A   E   6

You won't have any problems in this pairing, although the A won't always be able to understand the E. Because the A never plays any mind games, she or he finds it difficult to comprehend why someone else might. But the E is too guarded to feel comfortable exposing his or her true nature and often holds back. This might bother other partners a great deal, but fortunately the A is secure enough to generally be able to deal with the E's lack of emotional sharing.

| A   F | 7 |

The two of you are quite different from each other, but you each can accept the other and form a very loving union. The F is much more reserved than the A and won't communicate very readily. However, the A can gradually encourage the F to let loose and become more animated and spontaneous. Once the F comes out of his or her shell, he or she will be an enjoyable companion for the A.

| A   G | 10 |

A-G pairings are truly exhilarating. The A is full of energy and purpose when on his or her own, but becomes even more invigorated when paired with a G partner. The ambitious G has big dreams and will take the A along for the ride. There's no end to the fun and success you'll achieve together.

| A   H | 7 |

The H is not a perfect partner for the A, but the A is tolerant and level-headed enough to deal with the negatives of the relationship: namely, that the H is subject to frequent bouts of depression. Fortunately, the A's emotional stability and upbeat nature aren't adversely affected by these doom-and-gloom spells. In fact, the A can be extremely helpful in assisting the H to develop a happier perspective.

A   I   2

There are some basic problems inherent in your pairing. The I thrives on an extremely fast-paced life-style, whereas the A wants to live in a more balanced way, making time for the relationship and the simpler things of life. The A also will have some difficulty accepting some of the ruthless tactics that the I utilizes to get what she or he wants; this is completely contrary to the A's nature since the A is highly ethical and honest.

B   B   3

You'll share a wonderfully full social life since you both are highly gregarious. But you won't fare as well when you just spend time with each other. You both resent it when you're not the center of attention. Consequently, there will be frequent fights whenever you feel that the other person isn't being attentive enough.

B   C   7

Some people would find it difficult to be with a B partner, but the self-confident C doesn't mind the B's constantly trying to upstage him or her. The C is a go-getter who knows how to obtain what she wants out of life and isn't threatened by a partner like the B, who can get overbearing at times. Happily, you'll admire each other for your irrepressible spirit and spunk.

B D	1

The D's preference for privacy and a low-key life-style contrasts sharply with the highly social and flamboyant life-style favored by the B. You'll each need to make some compromises to reach a middle ground where you both can be comfortable. If you can do this, you'll enjoy an added dimension to your relationship and your individual lives as the D becomes somewhat less reclusive and the B learns to enjoy quiet contemplation and thoughtful introspection.

B E	9

The two of you are very compatible. You both basically have sunny, sociable natures and make friends easily. While you'll be in demand socially, you'll also want to spend some time alone so you don't lose touch on an intimate level with each other. This is particularly important for the E, who does suffer some insecurities and needs to know that his or her partner cares deeply.

B F	10

You each bring out the best in each other. The B helps the shy F to be more outgoing and better equipped for social situations. The F in turn brings a logical perspective and sound judgment into the relationship, thus enabling the often-impulsive B to avoid getting into trouble.

B G	9

Consider yourselves fortunate to be in a B-G pairing. You're both positive thinkers who want and expect the best out of life. The G can be somewhat of a workaholic at times, but the B can help temper this trait by showing the G how to relax and have fun. Conversely, the G's ambition and diligence will prevent the B from becoming too hedonistic and lazy.

B H	1

It often won't be easy for either of you to give the other what she or he needs. The H tends to become discouraged and depressed all too frequently. When this occurs, she or he needs a highly understanding partner. But the B typically is so concerned with his or her own self that the needs of a partner will go unrecognized. You'll both need to make some changes to improve your relationship. The H has to become more assertive about proclaiming what it is that she or he desires, and the B must become less self-centered. Once you modify your behavior, you'll be happier together.

B I	8

You'll often disagree on many issues, but you'll still make challenging partners for each other. The I respects the B's imagination and creativity, while the B admires the I's quick wit and intelligence. The highly perceptive and no-nonsense I can also keep the B in line whenever the B puts on too many airs or becomes too self-absorbed.

C C	5

Because you're both such strong personalities, there will be frequent clashes of wills. You believe in being assertive and don't readily give in to someone else's demands. If you can learn to successfully negotiate with each other when conflicts arise and develop win-win solutions, you'll have a happy and productive life together.

C D	3

The two of you have entirely different approaches to life. The C truly thinks of the world as his or her oyster, eagerly and confidently exploring all that it can offer. This is a definite contrast to the D, who wants to withdraw from the world as much as possible. For your relationship to succeed, it is imperative that the D give the C sufficient freedom; without it the C will feel too confined and restricted. The C needs to try to be very supportive so that the D develops more self-confidence.

C E	8

There won't be any major problems in your pairing. The E can be riddled with insecurity at times, but the self-confident C can help allay his or her fears. The C is typically goal-oriented rather than people-oriented; the E complements the C in this regard by having more of an interpersonal focus. So even though you're dissimilar personalities, you can be quite happy together.

	C F	8

The F is a very tentative person who often lets his or her fears prevent him or her from pursuing desired goals and experiences. But when combined with a C who is totally secure and fearless, the F can begin to become who she or he really wants to be. This relationship is obviously very beneficial to the F, but it can also be rewarding to the C, allowing him or her to be the helping partner and nurture someone else instead of getting too wrapped up in him- or herself.

	C G	10

Together the two of you will get everything you want out of life. Because you're both optimistic and determined, there is plenty of energy to devote to your pursuit of happiness. You're supportive of each other's efforts and will provide encouragement to reach for the stars. Other couples will envy you for all you achieve.

	C H	3

Because your energy levels are at opposite ends of the scale, you'll sometimes have difficulty relating to each other. The high-energy C doesn't acknowledge any barriers or obstacles in his or her life, whereas the H is usually too fatigued even to try to cope with adversity. If you want to make it as a couple, the H will need to try harder and give up less readily. The C in turn should refrain from continually pushing the H to accomplish more and instead provide gentle encouragement.

C I	6

The I is not the most tactful or openly affectionate person in the world, but the C is able to accept this. Because the C is secure and happy with him- or herself, he or she doesn't need a partner to constantly declare his or her love and commitment. Even when the I blurts out something thoughtless or even cruel, the C can handle it. You won't have as loving a relationship as some couples, but you'll at least be able to coexist fairly peacefully even if you don't connect on a deeply emotional basis.

D D	8

Two D's will have a very close relationship. You both tend to withdraw from the world at large, preferring to isolate yourselves. Consequently, you'll spend a great deal of time together, usually at home and with just the two of you. Some might say that your reclusive tendencies are unhealthy, but you know what's best for you and how you feel most comfortable.

D E	4

On the surface you appear to be moderately compatible. However, there will be some issues that need to be resolved for you to have a mutually fulfilling relationship. Unlike the more outgoing E, the D is not interested in anything other than his or her own small world. While the E may not mind the D's desire for privacy, she or he may have some difficulty coping with the emotional distance of the D. This trait of the D will always be present, but it need not destroy your relationship. If the E stops pressuring the D for more closeness and realizes that the D's undemonstrative nature doesn't mean an absence of caring, you can keep your relationship on the right track.

D	F		3

Y ou both need to resolve to help each other overcome your reserved natures. Without this commitment, you'll tend to reinforce your mutual tendencies to withdraw and avoid fully relating to another human being. If you let the F take the lead in gradually establishing a warm, giving, sharing relationship, the D will eventually feel less threatened about developing closer ties.

D	G		1

Y ou're basically as dissimilar as two people can be. The G sees everything with rose-colored glasses, while the D is suspicious and fearful of most everything in the world. The G wants to get all that she or he can out of life, whereas the D would rather withdraw and live in a very passive way. But it *is* possible to successfully merge your life-styles if you take advantage of your individual needs and differences. For example, the D can perform more of the homemaking tasks since she or he is most comfortable there, while the G goes out and conquers the world.

D	H		7

N either of you will do much to further the other's emotional, social, and intellectual growth. But this may be acceptable to you both. You'll tend to confine yourselves to each other rather than expand your network of friends and acquaintances. You'll also be likely to avoid trying new or potentially risky experiences. The advantage of your pairing, however, is that you'll be completely empathetic and supportive of each other.

D I	9

Although there are some differences between you, you can still relate well to each other. Other people might be put off by the I's cynicism, but the D tends to be less than optimistic and will be amused by the I's sardonic perspective. Because the I is somewhat disenchanted by the realities of life, she or he doesn't mind joining the escapist tendencies of the D. Together you'll establish a rewarding homelife and relationship.

E E	3

By nature, you're both affectionate and outgoing. But you also share a fear of intimacy. If things become too intense, one or both of you will withdraw and try to put some distance between you. Unless you put forth maximum effort to maintain open communication on a calm, rational basis, your relationship will be full of insecurity because you'll never quite know where you stand with each other.

E F	7

You are exact opposites. The E is gregarious while the F is introverted. What you do share is a lack of acceptance of your true natures. The E is afraid of getting hurt, so he or she tries to disguise how important other people are to him or her. The F, on the other hand, doesn't like being shy and wishes that he or she could relate more easily to others. Happily, when you combine forces, you just may be able to strike a happy balance between your two divergent temperaments and approaches.

F F	8

Although neither of you is the warmest person by nature, you share the desire to improve your ability to relate to others. Consequently, you'll both try very hard to communicate with each other in an open, honest way. You may not be demonstrative, particularly in public, but it will be obvious that there is a deep caring and commitment in your relationship.

F G	10

The G is an ideal partner for the F because she or he is so self-assured and socially competent. Whereas the F tends to feel ill at ease and hold back with other people, the G is not plagued by any insecurities and can show the F how to connect with the world around him or her. In return, the G will find that the F is an excellent helpmate and will empower the G to achieve his or her ambitious goals.

F H	2

While you happen to be somewhat alike, the F wants to break away from the anxieties and apprehensions that can become so restrictive. The F desperately wishes to change his or her personality so that he or she can have a more fulfilling life. It's essential that the H, even if resistant to making any changes of his or her own, support the F in taking charge of his or her life and allow the F to make any desired modifications. If the H is not willing to do this, the F is likely to become extremely dissatisfied.

E G	8

This is a good pairing. Some partners may not readily adjust to the E's neediness and insecurities, but the indomitable G takes it all in stride. You're both people-oriented, but you also care about achieving your nonhuman goals as well. Together you'll develop very satisfying social and work lives.

E H	7

The E is more of an upbeat personality than the H, but the E is good about toning down his or her natural exuberance so as not to overwhelm the H. While the H won't ever be very energetic, she or he may begin to follow the E's example and participate a little more in life. Yours won't be an especially dynamic relationship, but there won't be any major problems either.

E I	1

There is a propensity for a substantial amount of game-playing in your relationship. The E will often give mixed messages, sometimes behaving as if she or he desires a lot of intimacy and togetherness but at other times shying way from such closeness. The I will want to retaliate with his or her own version of playing "hot and cold." For your relationship to work, you need to break these patterns. Communicate with each other and let your true feelings be known. If one of you is unhappy or troubled, try to discuss it rather than send signals that may be misinterpreted.

| F   I | 9 |

You'll each be good for the other person. The F can be naive about other people and may lack the knowhow to survive in the world without getting stepped on, but the clever and assertive I can show him or her how to prosper and attain desired goals. The grateful F will reciprocate by trying to be as loving a partner as possible.

| G   G | 7 |

Out of all the couple combinations, a double-G pairing is the one that will achieve the most success in the world. You're both extremely ambitious and driven. There's no end to the amount of time and effort you'll devote to reaching your material goals. However, since any human being has only a finite supply of energy and time, you'll tend to neglect each other and the intimate aspects of your relationship.

| G   H | 1 |

You're as opposite of each other as night and day. The G will have difficulty understanding the H's lack of energy; the H will be overwhelmed by the seemingly inexhaustible drive and activity level of the G. The G will feel that the H is too pessimistic while the H won't readily relate to the G's upbeat mental attitude. For the sake of your relationship, you each will need to become more tolerant of the other. The G can begin to view the H as being intelligently cautious as the H develops more of an appreciation for the G's irrepressible determination to succeed in life.

G I	7

You can probably maintain a lasting (if somewhat distant) relationship. Neither the G nor the I is interested in constant companionship or deep communication. You both neglect your inner selves in favor of developing your outer personae. You're more interested in material advancement than in spiritual or emotional development. This would bother other partners, but the two of you prefer it this way and wouldn't want to change.

H H	2

As two H's, you will probably be together for a lifetime but mostly because you're too reluctant to make any changes in your lives. Even if you're not very happy with each other, you'll stay coupled rather than upset the applecart. But do recognize that you both need to strive to attain more positive attitudes. Be very careful not to reinforce your shared tendency toward depression.

H I	3

The two of you are worlds apart. The energetic I wants to be actively involved in a multitude of things, whereas the lethargic H prefers to exert as little effort as possible to get through life. To improve the outlook for your relationship, the I must try to help the H develop a more positive frame of mind. If she or he succeeds, the H will become a more stimulating and compatible partner for the I.

There will be frequent arguments in your relationship because you both lack the patience and compassion to try to fully understand the other person. But you'll still enjoy each other for the most part. One I will find another I to be a challenging partner whose quick mind enables stimulating conversations. You'll be able to achieve many if not all of your mutual goals because of your intelligence and energy.

4

Humor Appreciation

What is humorous to some people is not necessarily so to others. A joke that some people find funny will be incomprehensible or just plain boring to other people who hear it. Psychologists have studied this phenomenon, trying to learn what type of people enjoy which sort of humor. While there is no universal consensus on the various types of humor appreciation and their associated personality characteristics, it is possible to broadly classify senses of humor into four main categories. Take the short quiz below to classify your own senses of humor.

1. Which one of the following would be most likely to make you laugh?
  A Three Stooges
  B. A practical joke
  C. A joke book
  D. M*A*S*H
2. Where are you most likely to laugh?
  A. Comedy club
  B. Comic play
  C. At home, by yourself, reading the comics
  D. At home, with your partner, sharing a funny joke

3. Who do you think is the funniest of the following?
   A. Charlie Chaplin
   B. You
   C. Garfield the Cat
   D. Woody Allen
4. Which of these types of humor do you least like?
   A. Lengthy monologues dealing with the incongruities and absurdities of life
   B. Making fun of illness and death
   C. Live comedy routines
   D. Slapstick
5. Which is your favorite cartoon?
   A. Hagar the Horrible
   B. Cathy
   C. Doonesbury
   D. The Far Side

Person 1				
	A	B	C	D
Person 2				
	A	B	C	D

   Most people's answers will fall predominantly in one category (i.e. at least three out of five). If you find, however, that your answers are scattered fairly evenly among the four letters, read the following descriptions of the four types of humor appreciation and choose the one you feel best describes your own.

A — Enjoy slapstick.
   Enjoy ethnic jokes.
   Prefer short jokes and skits.
   Prefer to be around other people when enjoying comedy.
B — Enjoy practical jokes.
   Dislike black humor, satire, or other types of humor that may make people uncomfortable.
   Dislike ethnic jokes.
   Like comedy routines, plays, and movies.
C — Like cartoons.
   Generally prefer written humor to acted or spoken forms.
   Usually enjoy humor in a quiet way, not laughing uproariously or frequently.

D — Enjoy black humor
(*i.e.,* laughing at situations that aren't typically thought to be funny, such as death or illness).
Prefer very sophisticated humor.
Prefer written humor to all other types.
Dislike sex and aggression topics (*i.e.,* verbal attacks on others).

Pair your findings to learn whether your individual types of humor indicate an overall compatibility with each other.

Person 1	Type	Person 2
_____	A	_____
_____	B	_____
_____	C	_____
_____	D	_____

_____		_____
A A		1

You're very much alike, but don't automatically assume that this is advantageous for your relationship. You share feelings of inferiority about yourselves and attempt to deal with them by cutting other people down so you don't feel as if they're better than you. This obviously is not a constructive practice and you have to be careful not to deride each other. If you're going to ridicule or sabotage each other's efforts, you'll soon become adversaries rather than lovers. For any coupling to work well, it must be mutually supportive.

Another problem is your mutual impulsivity. Emotions rather than intellect will assume the dominant role in your relationship. There's a tendency to blurt out whatever's on your mind, even if it will be offensive or hurtful to your partner. To counteract this, you both need to take time to organize your thoughts and monitor your feelings. A loving relationship needs consistent kindness and compassion, so strive to make this a reality in your dealings with each other.

	A B	6

The B is just the type of partner that the A needs. The self-confidence of the B enables him or her to be content with who he or she is. Unlike the A, who can feel good about him- or herself only at the expense of someone else's well-being, the B feels best in a congenial, affirming atmosphere. The B will override the A's negativity and show him or her that happiness is possible only when everyone else is also happy. This will help the A become more sensitive and caring to a partner as well as to all the other people in his or her life.

With the A's aggressive tendencies under control, the two of you can have an enjoyable life together. You'll have lots of friends to socialize with, as well as many adventurous experiences. The restless nature of the A combined with the B's exuberance will probably lead to exciting travels, possibly even around the world. The two of you can make an indomitable team.

	A C	1

Both of you have a fair number of personal problems to work out. You experience a mutual tendency toward anxiety and insecurity. Your other shared characteristic is that of moodiness. These two traits make it difficult to be supportive of someone else. But it is absolutely necessary for you to look beyond your individual selves and current troubles if you want a loving relationship. With enough diligence, you each can achieve the relatively stable emotional state that is conducive to happiness as a couple.

You can also tackle your differing social needs with a similarly positive approach. While the C is a loner who is quite uncomfortable with social interaction, the A craves constant social involvement. The A will go to great lengths to be accepted by others whereas the C couldn't care less. There's no way to permanently resolve this major difference between the two of you, but continual compromise will go a long way in enabling you to satisfy your needs as individuals and as a couple. If the C agrees to participate in a few well-chosen social activities and the A will use more discretion in accepting invitations, the two of you can have a more harmonious relationship.

| A   D | 5 |

Although you're mirror opposites of each other, there is a good chance that your relationship will work. You can balance each other in a way few other couples can. The cautious D helps to keep the A's restlessness and impulsivity from getting completely out of hand; the A in turn assists the D in enjoying a little more spontaneity in life as opposed to being so overly cautious that she or he neglects to partake in unplanned (but ultimately very rewarding) experiences. The D has a definite tendency to become very sedentary and passive, but the A won't allow his or her partner to become too reclusive or inhibited.

Your emotional makeups are complementary. The D is stable and predictable, while the A's moods fluctuate readily. The A brings an emotional direction that would otherwise be missing in the D's life, and the D adds an intellectual element that is underdeveloped in the A. Together you can become more complete people than you could be separately.

| B   B | 6 |

A double-B pairing is nothing short of ideal. You both love life and have the energy to live to its fullest. Neither of you is a worrier; you tend to be extremely easygoing and turn even the most trying situations into something positive. The sensitivity of a B will ensure that both of you care deeply about the other's feelings. You'd never do anything to jeopardize your relationship.

You're both people persons and you relish the companionship of another B. One of your greatest pleasures is conversation. Two B's will be able to talk easily to each other and can be empathetic listeners as well. Communication will always be excellent between the two of you. Your mutual confidence in your individual selves and each other makes you secure and happy with the world and your place in it, allowing you to avoid the agony of soul-searching and instead concentrate on enjoying your lives together. Who could ask for anything more in a relationship?

B   C   **3**

If anyone can handle a C partner, it's a B. However, there will be times when the B will question what she or he is doing with the C. Because the B is so self-assured and secure, the C's free-floating anxiety doesn't really get the B down. But the B will not be happy with the C's reticence. The B wants a challenging conversational partner and the C, although intellectually capable of stimulating discussions, is too introverted to fully share his or her thoughts and, especially, feelings. The B's easygoing nature is at odds with the C's lack of flexibility and difficulty in taking pleasure in life.

But the B is extremely tolerant and can accept a lot of his or her partner's shortcomings, provided the C makes an honest effort to improve. The C isn't afraid of hard work and can strive to change some personality characteristics. It's most important for him or her to work on becoming a more open, sharing, giving partner. If she or he can do that, your relationship can be at least a moderate success.

B   D   **4**

There's no doubt that the two of you are different, but there's also no doubt that you appreciate your differences and admire the other for who she or he is. The B is a highly energetic, dynamic individual who is full of good ideas but doesn't always know how to put them into action. The D is a perfect mate for the D in this regard since the D is an expert planner who knows how to make things happen. If left to his or her own devices, the B might jump around from one activity to the next without ever seeing anything through to completion. The B would have big dreams but few of them would ever be realized. The D wouldn't be living a life because she or he would be too involved with analyzing everything and mapping out strategies for dealing with everything. But together you can accomplish great things.

The D is not very emotional, but is more comfortable with thinking than feeling. This is fine in his or her professional life but can be a little unnerving for the romantic partner. Fortunately, the B can accept this trait of the D without much difficulty. Other partners might perceive the D as being cold and uncaring, but the B is self-confident enough to realize that she or he really is loved by the D (even if not always in an outwardly demonstrative manner).

C C	2

A double C relationship requires a lot of hard work. Unless you make a conscious effort to avoid your mutual pessimism and anxiety, you'll tend to withdraw and avoid getting involved in life or with other people. Retreating together into your own little cocoon may feel safe, but it's not challenging. You both must resolve to encourage each other to at least occasionally explore what's outside your immediate world.

The other problem area is the tendency toward moodiness that you share. If you experience opposite moods at the same time (e.g., if one of you is anxious and agitated while the other is calm), this will negatively impact upon your ability to relate to each other. Learn to be flexible enough to cope with your partner's varying emotional states and behaviors, refraining from trying to get the other person to change his or her mood to suit your own. Accept each other's feelings, even if they make you uncomfortable at times.

| C   D | 5 |

The two of you are intellectual equals, and that can go a long way in keeping you satisfied with each other. You're both independent thinkers who don't need other people for mental stimulation or emotional satisfaction. Although the D is somewhat more people-oriented than the C, neither one of you will be clinging partners. You'll each feel free to be yourselves without worrying about what the other will think. Although you often don't connect emotionally, you'll know each other's thought processes well.

The D can be very beneficial for the C. All too often the C is paralyzed by anxiety and tends to withdraw from the world. But the D's cautious and rational approach can help the C gradually become a little more involved. While the D's analytical nature could become boring to a partner who is more action-oriented, the C will feel quite comfortable with it and will trust the D completely. You should have a stable, satisfying relationship together.

| D   D | 5 |

Your life together won't be exciting, but that suits each of you just fine. Neither of you wants to set the world on fire; you'd rather sit back and observe what goes on around you. But it's important to you both to have a sense of control over your immediate environment, so you carefully plan before taking any action. You study every situation in depth before even forming an opinion about it. Your lives may not be as full of activity as those of other couples, but you manage to keep each other intellectually stimulated. You see things with the same cynical perspective, and this enables you to fully share your thoughts with each other.

Together you'll have a sophisticated, intellectual life-style. Other people may criticize you for your lack of passion or risk-taking. This criticism may stem from jealousy or from a complete lack of understanding of who you are. Be true to yourselves and don't try to change anything about you. Your approach to life and love works for you both as individuals and as a couple, and that's all that matters.

5

Color Preference

What color do you most prefer? Color psychology research has shown that color choice offers revealing insights about an individual's personality. It can also help explore compatibility between two people, indicating strengths of the relationship as well as identifying potential sources of conflict.

To interpret what your color preferences say about your compatibility as a couple, each of you first needs to choose one of the following colors as your favorite. Do not spend a lot of time in making this decision; your first reaction is the most accurate. Don't take into consideration which color looks best on you or which one is used most in your home. Simply select the color that most appeals to you, then combine your answers and find your compatibility profile.

Person 1	Color	Person 2
_____	Red	_____
_____	Blue	_____
_____	Green	_____
_____	Yellow	_____
_____	Purple	_____
_____	Brown	_____
_____	Gray	_____
_____	Black	_____

NOTE: Your color preference may change from time to time, depending on your mood or events in your life, so you may want to select a color choice again at a later date. If you find it difficult to select just one color, ask yourself which color you would choose if you had to surround yourself (clothes and home decor) with just that one color. Still torn between two choices? You can check up to three. If, for example, you like both blue and green equally, put checks for both of these under your column. If your partner likes both green and red, these should be checked in his or her column. You'll then need to compare your answers three ways (green-green, blue-green, and green-red) and read the three different compatibility profiles. You may discover somewhat conflicting information from one profile to another, but this is to be expected since different aspects of your personalities are indicated by your preferences for more than one color.

RED   RED   **5**

When two reds are romantically involved, there's sure to be a great deal of excitement and intensity in the relationship. You both favor extremes and find anything middle of the road to be boring. Living to its fullest is your primary goal. You regret that there isn't enough time to take advantage of all the possibilities, but you make sure you experience as much as you can. Sitting on the sidelines is not for either of you; you'd rather participate in anything that promises to be interesting.

Is there a down side to this dynamic relationship? Unfortunately, there is. You share a tendency to be impulsive and may act in ways that could destroy your trust in each other. Your highly competitive natures can also lead to your resorting to less than loving means in your unrelenting determination to win. You both have strong personalities and each prefers to be the leader rather than a follower, so you have to expect a certain amount of discord as you both try to call the shots. Your relationship can definitely be exhausting at times, but it is almost always certain to be fulfilling.

RED BLUE	1

Red and blue can be a difficult pairing. The red is likely to try to dominate the blue and force him or her into a lifestyle that is far removed from what a blue would find comfortable. The quiet, stress-free life preferred by the blue is the exact opposite of the hectic, challenging, adventurous existence favored by the red. You can't even see eye to eye about your social life. The blue would much rather stay at home or visit a few close friends; the extroverted red always craves the excitement of meeting large numbers of new people.

But if you care deeply about each other despite your differences, you can make your relationship work. The key is providing each other with enough freedom to pursue your individual lives as you see fit. Allow the red some nights out on the town with friends while the blue relaxes at home. Let the blue have a room in the house that is serene and peaceful; another room can be decorated with the vibrant colors and lively decor that the red enjoys. If each of you can express your unique natures, you can live happily together.

| RED | GREEN | 4 |

Red and green are completely different from each other. The green's stable, well-balanced personality contrasts sharply with the erratic and extreme character traits of the red. The green is careful to logically and carefully map out his or her options, whereas the red acts on impulse. The social gregariousness of the red is not shared by the green, who cares deeply about others but is always too inhibited and concerned about what other people think to ever really let loose.

These differences notwithstanding, there can be some positive aspects to a red-green union. The red's emotional spontaneity and independence can help temper the green's worries about his or her image, allowing the green to experience the heady sensation of doing what he or she wants, regardless of what anyone else might think. The green can tone down the red's reckless behavior and possibly even prevent him or her from getting into serious trouble. Your relationship may have some ups and downs, but it can be worth preserving.

| RED | YELLOW | 5 |

What a great couple you two make! You both like to experience new things. The "same old same old" is deadly to both of you. As long as there's something different, trendy, or innovative, the red and yellow personalities are first in line to try it. Life can't help but be exciting when you're together. Your association is especially beneficial to the yellow partner, since he or she has a tendency to avoid making his or her dreams into reality, and the action-oriented red excels at *doing*.

But most relationships aren't perfect and yours has some problems as well. The more introverted yellow will be distressed with all the social stimulation that the red craves. The yellow is also likely to be unhappy with the red's impulsivity, since the yellow ponders his or her ideas before acting on them. To prevent these problems from hurting your relationship, you may need to have some separate leisure time in which the red can engage in extensive social interaction without the yellow's involvement. In addition, the red (with the yellow's guidance) will have to make a conscious effort to think before doing something that could hurt you as a couple.

RED PURPLE	2

Red and purple is a difficult combination. Both of you are prone to emotional extremes, fluctuating between exhilarating highs and devastating lows. You each need a partner who can serve as a stabilizing influence but you're not going to find it in either a red or purple personality. Another similarity between you is that you're both egotistical. Because you both want to be the center of attention, resentment flares when one of you is forced to relinquish the spotlight to the other. Rather than being supportive of each other's efforts and genuinely happy for your respective partner's triumphs, you may even try to sabotage the other person's success and happiness.

The only chance for your relationship succeeding lies with the purple partner. Since the purple is more passive than the red, she or he may be willing to allow the red partner to assume the more dominant role. Not every purple will be happy with this arrangement, but many purples have an active imagination and fantasy life. If the purple can escape from the harsh realities of your relationship by fantasizing, she or he may possibly be able to cope with the negative elements of a red-purple union while also developing some creative strategies for enhancing your life together.

RED BROWN	5

A red-brown relationship can be beneficial to both partners. If the conservative brown can maintain a sense of humor about the red's flamboyance, she or he may begin to enjoy life more. The red is an excellent partner for helping the brown to loosen up and not take things so seriously. The brown naturally feels more comfortable playing by the rules, but with the red's guidance she or he may see that some rules are made to be broken. On the other hand, the brown can help the red to become more disciplined and a little more down-to-earth. More than any other color, the brown can help to keep the red from getting into trouble through his or her wild, impulsive actions.

This is not to imply that all will be idyllic with your relationship. When two people are so different, there's bound to be some friction and misunderstandings. The red will be very tempted to break up your union when things get rough. Fortunately, the brown is highly committed to the idea of a stable relationship and can be counted on to do whatever it takes to keep your relationship going.

| RED   GRAY | 1 |

A successful relationship doesn't come easily to a red-gray couple. You really have to make a major commitment to ride out the rough times and try to understand each other. The emotionally detached gray will find it difficult to relate to the red's highs and lows. The red will probably find the gray too secretive and quiet. No matter how long the two of you are together, the red will often feel that she or he doesn't really know the gray at all. This will prove to be quite frustrating to the red, leading him or her to seek out other emotional outlets and friendships. The red's very full social life can further divide the two of you since the gray won't readily understand or approve of the red's need for other people.

Neither one of you should try to emulate the other. You each need to be your unique selves and not attempt to assume the other's personality. But if you want your coupling to last, some attitude adjustment is in order. Rather than seeing the gray as uninteresting and resenting him or her for not being a more stimulating companion, the red should begin to view the gray as someone who adds a little peace and tranquillity to an otherwise turbulent life. Instead of the gray becoming agitated by the red's unconventional and unpredictable behavior, the gray needs to realize that a totally stressless life holds no challenges and begin to appreciate the red more. The right perspectives will go a long way in improving your compatibility.

RED	BLACK		6

This is a match made in heaven! Red and black make a very dynamic duo. Both of you are nonconformists who aren't afraid to do the unexpected. No one tells either of you what to do, and you respect that in each other. You thus allow your respective partners to experiment and grow. Your creative juices really start to flow when you're together. You're admired as individuals, but especially envied as a couple for your sophistication and unique flair.

You might think that competition would be high in a relationship with two such strong personalities, but this is not the case. You're very supportive and proud of each other. You'll both put a lot of energy into the relationship to make it work. The black in particular will profit from this coupling, since she or he tends toward negativity, whereas the red has a more optimistic, affirmative outlook on life. Together you'll be able to keep your spirits high and make the most of your considerable personal attributes.

BLUE	BLUE		5

Both of you seek tranquillity and harmony in all aspects of your lives. You each tend to be more comfortable with a predictable, peaceful existence than with a life characterized by uncertainty and adventure. Arguments are rare; each of you will go out of your way to avoid any disagreements because you find them so stressful and upsetting. You share the same traditional tastes and wouldn't dream of experimenting with anything unorthodox or unknown. Loyalty is not a problem with you two. You want to be able to depend on the significant person in your lives, and your partner knows that she or he can count on you as well.

Unfortunately, your insistence on complete security (physical, emotional, and financial) can be extremely limiting. Rather than experiencing a variety of people and places, you tend to cling to those that are the most familiar. You are in definite danger of becoming stagnant as individuals and as a couple. In order to grow, you'll have to agree to take some risks and challenge each other to explore new things that will broaden your horizons.

BLUE	GREEN		5

Blue and green are very compatible. You can lead a predictable, stable life together. Other couples would be bored with your life-style, but neither of you enjoys drama or surprises. Both of you try to avoid emotional highs and lows, striving for an even keel at all times. Your conscientious natures ensure that you'll work hard to make your relationship a good one.

The only negative element in this otherwise happy union is the green's constant need for reassurance. The green's insecurity is apt to surface whenever she or he feels that the blue partner isn't being attentive enough. In actuality, the blue is a very caring, committed partner, but the green might not always perceive this. If the blue is ever preoccupied with his or her own concerns, the green will immediately feel neglected and make both of you miserable. The stress-free existence that both of you seek may be disrupted by this trait of the green, so it's crucial for the green to work through this problem by learning not to be so dependent and demanding.

BLUE	YELLOW		3

You have about a fifty-fifty chance for a happy relationship. One of the major factors affecting your compatibility is the differing needs you have for excitement versus serenity. The yellow thrives on a flashy, stimulating life-style full of new challenges and varied experiences. The blue is the exact opposite; she or he needs the security of a familiar emotional and physical landscape. Obviously you'll encounter problems in being together. This can range from such mundane details as choosing a videotape to rent (the blue wants to get a movie she or he has seen twenty times, whereas the yellow can't be happy unless it's the newest film out) to more significant concerns such as your home base (the blue needs to settle down permanently in one spot, while the yellow likes to experiment with living in different places).

Even with these potential areas of discord, it's possible for you to remain together. The idealistic yellow does care deeply about your relationship and will try hard to make it work. Also, the yellow has some highly innovative ideas but doesn't always act on them. A blue partner may give the yellow an excuse to lay some of these ideas to rest, since all this striving to keep current and be where the action is can be tiring to the yellow. With the blue's peaceful nature, the two of you may well be able to avoid too much emotional static in your relationship.

BLUE	PURPLE	1

It's impossible to deny your differences. The purple rides a perpetual emotional roller coaster, whereas the placid blue feels nothing is worth getting so upset about. In addition to the difference in your emotional styles, your social and political orientations are worlds apart as well. The blue is conservative; the purple is willing to try new approaches to a variety of situations.

Can your relationship continue under these circumstances? It can, but only if you're very tolerant of your divergent perspectives. Instead of being embarrassed by your respective partner's philosophy, learn to appreciate it for the insights it adds to your own frame of reference. Respect the other's needs and desires even if you can't totally identify with them. You'll never be clones of each other, but that shouldn't affect your ability to live and love together.

BLUE	BROWN	5

Blue and brown do well together. You both are very reliable and conscientious in your personal and professional lives. You're not interested in playing games; you relate to each other in a straightforward, honest manner. Neither of you is looking for excitement or glamour. You just want to live comfortably with partners you can depend on.

You both favor a conservative approach to everything you do, finding security in what's familiar to you. But occasionally you'll find yourselves unable to avoid the new, the unexpected, the nontraditional. When this occurs, you'll each have some difficulty

handling it. It may be wise to seek professional counseling in such
instances, since neither of you is equipped to deal with it. Both of
you will be so stressed by unplanned or innovative happenings that
you're likely to have difficulty relating to each other in a loving
manner. Recognize this potential Achilles' heel in your individual
selves and your relationship, and take constructive action to solve
the problem.

BLUE   GRAY   **4**

This is a good match in most aspects. Both of you favor
a low-key, tranquil life-style. You want to live quietly and safely in a
world you both frequently find threatening. Having a partner with
the same wants and needs is a source of comfort to both of you.
You would never deliberately do anything to jeopardize the peace
you've found together.

But at times you're not as good for each other as a nongray or
nonblue partner would be. The gray tends to be introspective,
almost to the point of being secretive. The blue may be unhappy
that you're not sharing as much as a couple. While the gray will
listen patiently to the blue's concerns, he or she rarely expresses
his or her own feelings. The blue may feel some insecurity as a
result of the gray's reticent nature. In addition, the blue is apt to
allow the gray to escape from life rather than encouraging partici-
pation in all the world has to offer. The gray is likely to retreat
farther into his or her own shell, and the blue may similarly
withdraw. To prevent this from becoming a major problem in your
lives, find some mutual friends or interests that will demand active
involvement in the outside world.

BLUE   BLACK   **1**

As opposites, you may initially be intrigued by your
differences. However, you may soon discover that your dissimilarities can lead to some problems. The blue needs a high degree of

security and tranquillity, but the black's boldness and fearlessness can pose a threat to the blue's comfort zone. The blue's desire for a peaceful life may never be realized with a black partner.

But there are advantages to your pairing. The black can provide the blue with some much-needed dynamism, coaxing the blue out of his or her placid but stagnant existence. The blue can help the black learn to cherish the existing world without always trying to tear it down and build it anew. Sharing a home and combining your lives will never be as smooth and effortless as it is for other combinations, but it can be beneficial for both of you.

GREEN GREEN	5

A double-green relationship should be as stable and well balanced as your personalities. You don't experience significant peaks and valleys; instead, you try to maintain a level of contentment every day of your lives. You make extremely loyal partners for each other. Because both of you are very conscientious, you'll expend great effort to make your home and shared life as happy as possible.

The only pitfall in this pairing is that you're both deeply concerned about what other people think of you. You always try to do what is socially correct and become overly involved in attempting to please others. Being people-oriented is a wonderful quality, but your need for affection can be overwhelming at times. There is nothing wrong with expecting each other to provide emotional support, but ultimately you will need to define and reinforce your individual selves. The world at large can't always do it for you, and neither can any one human being, no matter how sympathetic and supportive. Try to help each other become a little less emotionally dependent. Learn to affirm yourselves as worthwhile individuals and maintain these perceptions on your own rather than demand constant stroking from your partner, friends, and/or family.

| GREEN | YELLOW | | 6 |

Green and yellow complement each other nicely. You're both deeply caring individuals who can handle an intimate relationship well. The yellow is more of an innovator than the conformist green, who's happiest with the status quo, but this isn't a problem. Thanks to the yellow's vivacious personality and excellent communication skills, the green can be persuaded to partake of life a little more and experience new things. The green tends to be insecure and is constantly worried about what others think of him or her, but the yellow is less concerned about social perceptions and can teach the green to be true to him- or herself.

This is not to imply that the benefits of a green-yellow coupling are one-sided. To the contrary, the green can have just as positive an impact on the yellow's well-being. The yellow may tend to go off on tangents, placing undue emphasis on one area of his or her life and neglecting the other parts. The green is the perfect partner to help the yellow develop a more balanced life-style. The green's conscientious, diligent nature can also teach the yellow to thoroughly complete his or her projects and responsibilities instead of never really following through with them to their logical conclusion. In short, cherish this relationship . . . it's a terrific one!

| GREEN | PURPLE | | 3 |

Yours is by no means an ideal combination, but it may be workable. Much of its ultimate success or failure will depend on the green partner. If the green can get over his or her considerable insecurity, he or she may be able to accept the purple's mood swings. But if the green continues to need constant reassurance, he or she will have difficulty dealing with the purple and is likely to take it personally when the purple becomes depressed or withdrawn. More often than not, the purple's funky mood may have nothing to do with the green, but the green will be convinced that it does and will become despondent as well.

But if the green is willing to work through this anxiety, this can have a very positive influence on the purple. In fact, if you stay together long enough, the purple may become more emotionally stable and begin to function more like the serene green. The purple can liven up the complacent life of the green and expose him or her to new worlds that the green would never experience if left to his or her own devices.

GREEN BROWN	6

The two of you are nearly identical! You're both conservative and believe in playing by the established rules. You're both honest and down-to-earth. You share the same priorities in life: a comfortable home, a stable romantic commitment, and a willingness to work hard to make it all come together for you. Compassion and caring are an intrinsic part of both of you, and you bring this out even more intensely in each other.

On his or her own, the brown may tend to be somewhat humorless and almost takes life too seriously. But a green partner will enhance the brown's vitality, adding a gentle spark to what would otherwise be a drab brown existence. The green can do this for the brown without even trying, since you're both in perfect synchrony with each other. In return, the brown never gives the green a moment's worry. The green can easily have the peaceful life she or he desires, content in unconditional and irrevocable love of the green. With a match like this, why would either of you ever want to end the relationship?

GREEN GRAY	4

Your relationship can be successful once you work out a few details. You're similar in lots of ways. You're both loyal, dependable, and emotionally stable. Neither of you is out to set the world on fire. You'll leave fame and fortune to your more ambitious friends. As long as you can share a quiet life with a compatible partner, each of you is happy. But the green is far more social than the gray and this can present some problems. The green may feel that the gray cramps his or her social life, and the gray may view the green's friends as an intrusion on your life together. In addition, the green may become anxious when the gray gets into one of his or her uncommunicative moods. Although the gray really hasn't given the green any reason to doubt his or her commitment to the relationship, the green is insecure enough to believe that the gray wants out when involved in his or her own world and isn't very attentive.

Learn to compromise in regard to your differing needs. Plan for some group gatherings that will serve as a social outlet for the green, but arrange for an equal amount of time together for just the two of you. After the gray works through one of his or her introspective periods, openly discuss your feelings about what occurred. If the gray is willing to share with the green what she or he was experiencing, the green may be better equipped to cope the next time the gray withdraws. The green needs to tolerate the gray's occasional need for some private time to deal with his or her emotions. Accepting your respective partner's social and emotional style is the key to making the most of this relationship.

| GREEN | BLACK | | 1 |

There are several things that draw you together. The green can't help but admire the black's sophistication. Since the green cares so deeply about his or her public image, it is gratifying to have such an impressive partner as the black. Naturally, the black doesn't mind having a partner who idolizes him or her. Together you'll have an enviable social life. The black is a trendsetter and leader who draws people like a magnet, while the green brings a natural affinity for friendship and cultivates close ties with a variety of people.

But without careful monitoring, your relationship can experience several pitfalls along the way. You're likely to become so involved with other people that you may neglect each other. In the midst of being social butterflies, you might forget about the people who you care for most deeply. The only solution is to regularly set aside time for you to be alone together so you don't lose touch with each other.

Another problem can be that the green, though initially reveling in the black's take-charge attitude and energetic personal style, may come to resent being dominated so completely by the black. To prevent this from escalating to a point of no return, the green needs to become more assertive and less willing to let the black always have the upper hand. If you both make a consistent effort to treat each other as equals and make time for your relationship, you'll do better as both friends and lovers.

YELLOW	YELLOW	5

You share identical character traits. You both enjoy things that are new, different, futuristic. Rather than feeling threatened by change, you yearn for it. As far as you're concerned, the "same old thing" is boring and unchallenging. You prefer stretching your intellects and your imaginations to the limit. You're both extremely idealistic and would like to help make the world a better place. While you enjoy material things, they're not nearly as important to you as are the more spiritual aspects of life.

Sound good so far? It should! A double-yellow relationship can be wonderful. But there is one thing to watch out for. That yellow idealism is seldom translated into concrete action. The two of you would rather contemplate your ideas than actually test them out. Consequently, many important things that you'd like to accomplish as a couple will never come to fruition. To avoid the unsettling realization years from now that time has sped by and you haven't done half of what you intended to, you'll need to make a concerted effort to motivate each other to become doers rather than just thinkers and dreamers.

YELLOW	PURPLE	4

Expect an interesting relationship when yellow and purple come together. You're two of the most creative individuals around, with a distinct flair for the innovative and the artistic. Your highly developed imaginations ensure that you'll continually come up with ways to make your relationship special. Whether you've been together two months or twenty years, there will always be a sense of excitement that you create together.

But you're by no means a perfect match. You each have your shortcomings, and there will inevitably be some problems in your combined lives. The purple's moodiness can be difficult for the yellow to tolerate. The yellow is deeply committed in theory to sharing his or her partner's ups and downs but in reality has trouble coping with someone else's turmoil and can become a little stand-offish when the purple's volatility becomes too taxing. The yellow may also be resentful of the purple's attempts to dominate and be the boss of the relationship. Furthermore, you're both prone to live in a fantasy world where you weave wondrous dreams but don't accomplish anything in real life. These problems can't be easily resolved. But if you can accept these flaws in an otherwise enjoyable pairing, you will find great satisfaction in being together.

| YELLOW | BROWN | | 6 |

In your case, opposites do attract and can be very good for each other! The brown is much more conservative than the yellow, but you can usually manage to merge your divergent philosophies and styles. The yellow's fascination with the new can be tempered by the brown's stubborn clinging to the old . . . and together you'll create a shared perspective that will be better than anything either of you would have had separately. Another area of mutual benefit is your work orientations. The brown believes that extreme diligence is constantly necessary in life, whereas the yellow is more playful and less hardworking. Without the brown, the yellow might never get anything done; with the yellow's help, the brown learns to loosen up and enjoy the world as it is rather than looking at it as a ruthlessly demanding taskmaster who assigns never-ending chores and responsibilites. Futhermore, the brown cares deeply about those people who are closest to him or her and can show the yellow how to be more openly affectionate.

If you're looking for any negatives in this relationship, you'll be sorely disappointed because there aren't any. Yellow and brown are simply a wonderfully compatible combination in every possible way.

YELLOW	GRAY	2

It's up to the two of you to determine the fate of your relationship. A yellow-gray coupling can be a happy, long-term union or a short-lived, traumatic association. It's a given that you're very different from each other. You need to decide whether you're going to let these differences tear you apart or not. The major issue is the way each of you relates to the outside world. The gray prefers to retreat as much as possible, particularly when things get too tumultuous; the yellow favors more active involvement. It is not surprising, therefore, that the gray is very much a loner while the yellow thoroughly enjoys social interaction.

Although it would appear that your styles are too far apart to ever make peace with each other, this doesn't have to be the case. With a little attitude adjustment, you can begin to appreciate your respective partners for what they are rather than what they're not. Instead of the yellow's bemoaning the gray's reticence, she or he can look upon the gray as a gentle, calming influence. Rather than fighting the yellow's upbeat, adventurous personality, the gray can allow the yellow to end the self-imposed isolation and may actually find that the gray enjoys the social stimulation (in small doses). If you have open minds, you very well might discover that your differences should be savored rather than suffered.

YELLOW	BLACK	3

Your relationship has some potential, but it won't always be easy. There will be a clash of wills on occasion. The yellow isn't quite as domineering as the black, but neither does she or he want to play a totally passive role. While the black is the more active partner who makes things happen, the yellow has a mind of his or her own and doesn't want to have ideas imposed by someone else. Fortunately, your interests and values are quite similar for the most part. You both want to make an impact on the world, you each enjoy exploring new horizons, and the two of you tend to become easily dissatisfied with anything that isn't entirely to your liking.

You do need to be aware of your shared tendency to view things in a negative light. When left to his or her own devices, the yellow will question whatever doesn't seem right and will then plan strategies for resolving the problem (although these strategies are typically never implemented because the yellow is more of a thinker than a doer). The black's influence may cause the yellow to dwell even more on all the things that are wrong in the world in general and the yellow's life in particular. This unhappy preoccupation can lead to the yellow becoming depressed and completely ineffectual in improving his or her life. Having a partner in such a frame of mind obviously does nothing positive for the black's morale. To avoid sinking into a life filled with despair and gloom, both of you need to try harder to focus on the positive.

PURPLE   PURPLE   4

A double-purple relationship will be filled with drama. Neither of you is inclined to fade into the background. You both know you have a lot going for you and you see no reason not to flaunt it. Other people may criticize you for your bold personal styles and egos, but this doesn't bother you at all. You have each other as well as a healthy dose of self-confidence, so you wouldn't dream of toning down your personalities.

But lest you think that everything is perfect when two purples are romantically involved, consider this. You share a definite tendency to prefer a fantasy world to real life. You could easily find yourselves becoming escapists who can't deal with reality. Due to your restless, changeable natures, you may find it difficult to make a long-term commitment. You tend to dislike obligations and prefer to live with as much freedom as possible, but any relationship will involve some loss of freedom along with the need to compromise. It's crucial that both of you develop some coping mechanisms that enable you to deal with the responsibilities and realities of your lives.

| PURPLE   BROWN | 6 |

You don't share any personality traits, but this doesn't make you incompatible. To the contrary, you each manage to complement the other in very positive ways. The purple's vivaciousness offers a welcome contrast to the brown's more restrained nature. Rather than the purple competing for the spotlight with a more dynamic partner, the brown happily fades into the background so that the purple can receive the attention she or he craves. The purple's presence prevents the brown from falling into a monotonous life-style, bringing an element of surprise and challenge into the brown's predictable existence.

Each of you is exactly what the other needs. The purple's imagination and creativity enable the brown to escape from a syndrome of all work and no play. While the brown tends to be happy and content regardless of the particular details of his or her life, the purple can significantly enhance the brown's pleasure. The brown returns the favor by giving the purple unconditional acceptance. This allows the purple to feel free to experiment with his or her creative urges, since the tolerant brown won't pass judgment. The brown may not be the most interesting partner, but it's actually a relief for the purple to share his or her life with a low-key, undemanding person. Both the brown and purple should find much satisfaction in this union.

| PURPLE   GRAY | 1 |

A purple-gray relationship can be a rocky one. A purple partner is inclined to prevent the gray from achieving the stressless existence she or he finds so appealing. The combination of the purple's ego, fluctuating temperament, and penchant for drama can be overwhelming for the gray. The gray is happiest when allowed to fade into the background, but the boisterous purple makes it impossible for the gray to neatly retreat when things get to be difficult to deal with. Because the purple won't allow the gray to remain isolated and passive, the gray is forced to live a purple life-style, which makes him or her uncomfortable.

But if the purple can be a little less zealous about making the gray over in more of a purple image, things will go more smoothly. Instead of trying to change the gray into a gregarious and creative individual, the purple needs to realize that the gray actually complements rather than hinders the purple personality. The gray won't try to compete with the purple; she or he much prefers to stay out of the limelight rather than doing anything that would steal attention away from the purple. In turn, the gray should learn to appreciate the purple's passion and exuberance. A purple partner will ultimately enrich the gray's life, making it fuller and more challenging. After some serious thinking about your relationship, you'll probably conclude that your differences may be substantial but not necessarily negative.

| PURPLE | BLACK | | 3 |

Never a dull moment in this relationship! You both think highly of yourselves and consequently feel that you deserve to get everything you want. These feelings of self-worth and entitlement result in some aggressive actions to obtain whatever it is you desire. At times you're likely to find yourselves competing in less than loving ways to satisfy your needs. A purple-black coupling will experience many struggles for power. Both of you would like to be the leader rather than merely being one half of the team. The black is even more domineering and determined than the purple, so is apt to win these contests for control. If the purple can learn to accept this, the relationship may survive. But if the purple refuses to assume a somewhat passive role, the two of you will experience a war between two strong personalities rather than a loving union.

However, all is not negative in your relationship. Together you achieve a high degree of cultural and social sophistication. You both rise above the mundane life-styles of other couples by embracing whatever is new, creative, or challenging. Your many admiring acquaintances don't suspect that you fight so furiously in your private life; all they know is what you present in public, and they find it very impressive. In reality, you lack the warmth that other, more compatible couples enjoy, but you can relish the glamorous image you present as a couple.

BROWN   BROWN   4

Other couples may have more fun, but the two of you have the last laugh when it comes to material success. You can set ambitious goals together and easily reach them. While other, more frivolous couples are floundering at their jobs or are even experiencing financial distress, you two will do extremely well. Each of you is a role model for the other. If you're ever tempted to be a little less diligent and conscientious, another brown individual is just the person to get you back on track.

The trouble is that neither of you knows how to enjoy your success. You're likely to accumulate great amounts of wealth but never really spend it in a way that brings you happiness. The serious, disciplined natures that you share have prevented you from experiencing the joy of life. A vicious cycle is apt to occur in a double-brown relationship: you work and worry so much that you never learn how to play, and then because you don't know what to do with leisure-time you end up working even harder to fill up the emptiness. The two of you will never know what it's like to enjoy life and each other unless you resolve not to be quite so structured all the time. Even if just once a week, let yourself go. Instead of always devoting yourselves to work, apply that same determination to having fun.

BROWN   GRAY   6

A brown individual is as perfect for the gray as the gray is for the brown. There's no question about your compatibility! You both want a dependable partner to share a quiet life together. Neither of you would be tempted for even a moment to find a more exuberant or innovative companion. You'd never want to sacrifice the comfort and security of your stable life-style.

You shouldn't experience any problems in this relationship as long as things continue at the steady, predictable pace you're both so comfortable with. As long as you can avoid any changes in your routine, you'll enjoy a tranquil existence. But beware of how you'll fare as a team if you ever face any significant changes or hardships.

Since you've never developed the inner strength or coping mechanisms to deal with upsets to your shared life, you may find what you've built together can be easily torn apart.

BROWN   BLACK   1

There will be frequent occasions where the two of you won't see eye to eye. The black likes nothing better than tearing down the old to bring in whatever is new, whereas the brown clings to familiar patterns. The black will sometimes experiment with new methods and styles just for shock value; the brown isn't very receptive to even considering that anything could be better than the traditional ways. Instead of compromising, the assertive black will usually try to inflict his or her way on the good-natured brown partner.

But compromise is absolutely essential for the survival of your relationship. The brown needs to become more open to change. This will be uncomfortable at first for him or her, but the brown will soon learn to enjoy the novelty of trying new things. Little by little, the brown will come to appreciate the black for keeping life interesting rather than safe but boring. As for the black, he or she needs to make some modifications in his or her attitude and behavior as well. The black needs to take care not to push the brown too far or too quickly since the only way a brown can deal with change is gradually. The black must also fight a natural tendency to take advantage of the brown. Making these changes won't be easy for you, but they'll enable your relationship to succeed.

GRAY   GRAY   3

You won't experience many problems together, but you also won't experience a very dynamic life. That's acceptable to both of you since you prefer lives that are consistently free of stress. In trying to avoid the struggles and upsets that are an inherent part of life, you may be limiting your opportunities for growth and fulfillment. You might avoid pain along the way, but you're also likely to detach yourselves from the challenges and rewards that life can offer.

Unlike other couplings, a gray-gray relationship won't have any competition or confrontation. You both tread quietly and cautiously through life. But a double-gray relationship sacrifices intimacy and communication. Each of you is self-contained; you don't see any need to outwardly express your emotions. Since you both share this trait, it's not threatening to either of you. Unfortunately, however, warmth will be lacking in your interaction with each other. At times you may find yourselves questioning whether you're together because of a deep love or simply because you're so comfortable with each other at this point that you're hesitant to look for more exciting partners.

| | GRAY   BLACK | 1 |

For gray and black to be even minimally compatible, a great deal of hard work will be required. The black may tend to feel dragged down by the gray. Whenever the gray opts for withdrawing from troubling events and issues, the black's naturally rebellious nature kicks in. The black then wants to become even more actively involved in meeting these challenges head-on. Because the black will push the gray to partake in aspects of life she or he would rather retreat from, the gray will become even more withdrawn in self-defense.

Obviously this cycle needs to be broken if you both want a satisfactory relationship. You each need to adjust your attitudes for the sake of the other. The black needs to tone down his or her tendency toward negativity; the gray must decrease his or her pessimistic views. This will make you happier as individuals and as a couple. It's also important that the black refrain from ruthlessly forcing the gray to do anything that makes him or her uncomfortable. The black can't expect the gray to keep up with him or her in all aspects of life together. The gray is not supposed to be the black's shadow, but a person in his or her own right who is entitled to have needs and desires that differ from those of the black. Accept these differences as a natural part of your relationship so that you can be at peace with each other.

BLACK   BLACK   4

Your complex relationship will often be difficult, but it's one that you shouldn't give up on too easily. When a dual-black relationship works, it can be very satisfying. The two of you are such dynamic and strong personalities that you could overwhelm less forceful partners. Together you can enjoy a sophisticated lifestyle filled with exciting new experiences.

The things that make you so interesting as individuals can interfere with your ability to function as a couple. You're both rebellious, particularly when you can't identify with a point of view that is different from your own. Both of you want to be in control and have the upper hand in the relationship. You tend to become very unhappy when the events and people in your lives fall short of the ideal you had in mind. All these traits are responsible for your frequent arguments. But you do understand each other far better than a nonblack partner ever could, and you'll find that all the turmoil is worth putting up with because your good times can be so spectacular.

6

Sleep Position

You may think you're not revealing your personality as you sleep, but nothing could be farther from the truth. Even though you may not be talking or interacting with anyone, the sleep position(s) you assume reflect a great deal about the person you are in your waking hours.

An individual may sleep in a dozen different positions, but some are assumed for only short periods of time. Most of us have one or two positions in particular that we favor. It is easy enough to pinpoint your customary position. If you aren't sure about it, ask someone to observe you while you sleep.

Read the following descriptions of sleep positions and characterize your individual types. Psychiatrist Samuel Dunkell, expert in the field and author of *Sleep Positions: The Night Language of the Body* (New York: Morrow, 1977), considers the fetal, semifetal, supine, and prone positions to be the most common (but notes that there are variations of these, depending on the placement of the hands and feet, for example). Once you both have determined your favored position(s), compare your answers to learn what your sleep postures say about your compatibility as a couple.

Fetal

Sidelying, body curled up, knees bent and drawn up toward the chin, hands clutching the knees or folded across the center of the body

Semifetal

Sidelying, with knees partially drawn up, possibly resting head on one arm; a modification of the fetal, without being curled as tightly

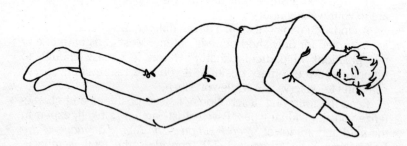

Supine
  Lying on the back, legs straight and apart, arms straight and away from body

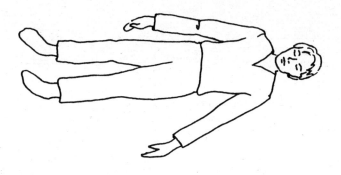

Prone
  Lying on the stomach, arms extended past head, legs stretched out, feet apart

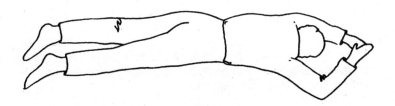

Person 1	Position	Person 2
_____	Fetal	_____
_____	Semifetal	_____
_____	Supine	_____
_____	Prone	_____

NOTE: You may find that you favor more than one position. For example, you may start off by falling asleep in the supine position but then wake up in the semifetal. The best position to choose for the sake of this quiz is the one you actually sleep in rather than the one in which you fall asleep. But if you use more than one position during the night, put a check by each one. You'll then need to look up the profiles for each possible pairing. For example, if you're both fetal and prone and your partner is supine, you'll read the profiles for fetal-supine and prone-supine.

FETAL   FETAL   **5**

Because you both want exactly the same things from your relationship, you'll make sure that all your mutual needs are fulfilled. You'll aim for a structured, predictable life-style that makes you feel secure. You'll be very dependent on each other and will be hesitant to let other people into your lives because you're not sure whether they're trustworthy. You're both fearful of the unknown and will do whatever you can to avoid it. As long as you're together, your individual growth will be restricted, but this prospect provides comfort rather than dismaying you.

| FETAL | SEMIFETAL | 5 |

The well-adjusted semifetal sleeper makes an excellent partner for the fetal sleeper. Since the semifetal sleeper is at peace with him- or herself, he or she is well able to cope with the fetal's insecurities and help allay some of them. While the fetal will always be a little reluctant to fully participate in life, the semifetal's patient understanding and encouragement will enable the fetal to gradually develop a fuller life.

| FETAL | PRONE | 5 |

The two of you are very compatible. You both like to organize your lives to avoid the unexpected. You're both willing to sacrifice a great deal of personal freedom for the sake of security. The prone sleeper is slightly more active and assertive than the fetal partner, but this works out well since the fetal sleeper is perfectly happy to let the prone partner assume the leadership role in the relationship.

| FETAL | SUPINE | 1 |

Proceed carefully in this pairing because the two of you are very different. The supine sleeper is extremely self-confident and secure in his or her place in the world. He or she thrives on lots of attention and admiration from others. But the fetal sleeper is just the opposite. He or she prefers to live in a retiring, passive manner, shrinking into the background as much as possible. Some simple measures will need to be taken to ensure that both of you feel comfortable in the relationship. The supine will need to make sure that the fetal doesn't drag him or her down. It's important that the supine pursue activities regardless of whether or not the fetal is willing to join him or her. It's equally crucial that the fetal stand up for his or her own rights and live the way he or she deems best, even if the supine thinks it unhealthy. But don't just resort to living your own separate lives. Be sure to find activities you can enjoy together even if it requires a lot of analyzing and negotiating to determine some possibilities.

| SEMIFETAL   SEMIFETAL | 6 |

Perfection in any relationship may not be a reality, but yours comes as close as is humanly possible. You share excellent mental health and you both relate to the world in an open, joyful manner. You're receptive to anything that will bring happiness into your lives. You'll encourage each other to embrace change and new experiences that will make your lives even more fulfilling. You've accepted who you both are and don't try to torture yourselves with trying to be something that you're not.

| SEMIFETAL   PRONE | 4 |

Thanks to the semifetal's easygoing attitude, your relationship shouldn't have too many problems. Other individuals might resent the prone partner's obsession with details and the way the prone partner attempts to dominate, but the semifetal sleeper can take this in stride. If the prone partner becomes too overbearing and rigid, the semifetal sleeper will speak up and work with the prone sleeper to change his or her ways. But, for the most part, the semifetal sleeper will look upon the prone partner's personality quirks with affection and a sense of humor.

SEMIFETAL	SUPINE	6

Yours will be a great relationship. The semifetal sleeper doesn't share the supine's constant need to be in the limelight and will refrain from competing for the number-one spot. Because the semifetal partner can be supportive of the supine sleeper's needs, the supine partner will appreciate the semifetal personality. The two of you won't be working at cross-purposes because you basically want the same things out of life: sufficient challenges and adventures to keep growing as individuals.

PRONE	PRONE	2

It's inevitable that there will be frequent power struggles in your relationship. Both of you feel the need to be in control, but it won't always be possible for you to take charge. Rather than yielding gracefully, you're both apt to resort to any means necessary to be in command. You'll behave as adversaries as often as you'll act as lovers.

PRONE	SUPINE	3

Although the prone sleeper might sometimes wish for a passive partner whom she or he could influence and dominate, the supine sleeper is by no means unassertive and pliable enough to be manipulated by anyone. To the contrary, the supine personality is extremely strong, self-confident, and unafraid. If the prone sleeper insists on dominating his or her partner, the supine will grow increasingly unhappy and will eventually want to terminate the union. It's therefore crucial that the prone learn to consider and treat the supine as an equal. If the prone sleep partner decides that she or he can live with the supine sleeper being his or her own person, you can have a satisfactory relationship.

SUPINE   SUPINE   5

Each of you wants to be the star in your relationship. It's not a question of wanting power so much as craving attention and admiration. There will be a great deal of competition between the two of you, but you should be able to keep this on a healthy level. By combining your strong personalities and mutual talents, you'll be sure to have a stimulating life together.

7

Exercise Preference

Everyone agrees that regular exercise is crucial to mental and physical health. But there's no universal consensus as to the best form of exercise. Some people advocate one type of exercise, whereas others are firmly convinced that *their* type is the most beneficial and enjoyable.

The exercise form that each of you chooses can say a lot about your compatibility as a couple. For example, the dynamics of a couple who both prefer swimming are different from those of a couple in which one partner favors weight training and the other walking. Compare your individual exercise preferences so that you may discover what your choices reveal about your relationship.

Quiz

Which of these types of exercise is the one you most frequently perform? If you're not currently exercising, pick the one you last did or would be most likely to do in the future. After each of you makes a selection, combine your answers and locate the section that discusses your paired exercise preferences.

Person 1	Exercise Preference	Person 2
_____	Running	_____
_____	Bicycling	_____
_____	Swimming	_____
_____	Walking	_____
_____	Yoga	_____
_____	Exercise class	_____
_____	Martial arts	_____
_____	Weight training	_____
_____	Tennis/Racquetball	_____
_____	Ballet/Figure skating	_____

N O T E : It's easiest if you can choose only one type of exercise as the one you prefer over all others. However, if you like two or three different forms of exercise and just can't pick one, you can check off up to three under your column. You'll then need to compare these choices to your partner's, taking into account all possible combinations. For example, if you like running and swimming and your partner likes martial arts, yoga, and swimming, you'll need to look up the profiles on running-martial arts, running-yoga, running-swimming, swimming-martial arts, swimming-yoga, and swimming-swimming. With this many profiles, you'll find some contradictory information. Your swimming-martial arts pairing may be a wonderful combination, whereas your running-martial arts coupling may indicate the potential for problems in your relationship. This information can all be valid since it can pinpoint the different dynamics that may go on in your relationship at different times.

RUNNING	RUNNING	5

Y ou're very well matched . . . perhaps overly so. Both of you are extremely ambitious, always putting your respective careers before your relationship. This could lead to some problems since it takes a great deal of time and effort to sustain a relationship. Fortunately, you both are experts at setting goals and reaching them. If you find that you're drifting apart, you can easily analyze your problems and pinpoint strategies for enhancing your life together. You each have the determination and focus to do whatever is necessary to get your partnership back on the right track.

RUNNING	BICYCLING	5

A lthough you're as different from each other as night and day, bikers and runners can be quite compatible. The biker is much more traditional than the runner, preferring to stick with the familiar. The runner, on the other hand, likes things to be continually new and exciting. This won't be a problem if you compromise and strive to find a mutual comfort zone. The self-confidence of the runner can rub off onto the biker, thus boosting his or her morale. The runner can learn to appreciate the calm predictability associated with the biker and develop a less frenetic and, possibly, more satisfying life-style.

RUNNING	SWIMMING	6

A runner and swimmer each bring unique qualities to a relationship. You make a very special couple. The swimmer has a sensual approach to life, thoroughly relishing pleasurable experiences of all kinds. The runner, on the other hand, is frequently too busy speeding through life and too preoccupied with his or her own concerns to take full advantage of life's offerings. The swimming partner can help the runner learn to relax and enjoy the journey rather than just the destination. The goal-oriented runner can help the swimmer overcome his or her lazy streak by motivating the swimmer to become more energetic so you become more productive both as a couple and as individuals.

RUNNING	WALKING	6

With mutual respect, your relationship can flourish for a lifetime. The runner's fast-paced, almost compulsive nature is markedly different from that of the walker, but the runner can easily appreciate the walker's steadiness. The runner can't help but admire the practical, dependable style and inner strength of the walker. Although the walker may appear quiet and unassertive, he or she knows exactly who he or she is and wants to do things his or her own way. The runner needs to resist the temptation to try to make the walker over in his or her own image. If each of you is allowed to be yourself, you'll be certain to stay a happy, well-adjusted couple.

RUNNING	YOGA	4

The two of you don't have much in common. The partner who practices yoga is very inner-directed and spiritual, while the runner is externally oriented and focuses on the material world. The runner is highly competitive, whereas the yoga partner prefers to quietly and peacefully coexist with others. The runner wants a fast-paced, fast-track life-style; the yoga partner seeks a much slower tempo. It would be unrealistic to expect either of you to change to suit the other person. Nonetheless, you *can* make a go of your relationship. The yoga's patience enables him or her to cope with the runner's relentless striving and constant activity. In addition, determination and goal-orientation empower the runner to commit to the relationship and do everything possible to make it succeed.

RUNNING	EXERCISE CLASS	2

Yours is a difficult coupling. You're both extremely competitive and can sometimes find yourselves working against each other rather than together for your mutual benefit. Both of you crave constant sensory stimulation, often leading to a mental overload. You both are likely to get involved in too many activities that deplete your physical and emotional reserves. Another complicating factor is that the runner is less of a social being than the partner who participates in exercise classes. The exercise class partner may become frustrated by the runner's need for private time and will tend to feel neglected. This will be a continuing problem in your relationship unless the exercise class partner learns to become more independent.

RUNNING	MARTIAL ARTS	3

You're both independent, practical people, but the similarity ends there. The partner who practices martial arts is much more introspective than the runner. The running partner tends to be externally driven and single-minded. The martial arts partner may find the runner's style to be somewhat superficial and shallow. Naturally, this can ultimately prove destructive to your relationship. But it *is* possible for the runner to become more inner-directed, particularly when she or he has a martial arts partner who can set an example and help focus on a deeper, more meaningful way of life.

RUNNING	WEIGHT TRAINING	2

It's difficult for both partners to be satisfied in this relationship because each of you is often too wrapped up in your individual self to give a partner what she or he needs. The runner doesn't want to be tied down to a demanding partner, but prefers a great deal of freedom in a relationship. The weight trainer needs a lot of emotional stroking, a need that the runner may not always be able to satisfy. Some changes are needed on both your parts. If the weight training partner can understand that the runner really has a lot of respect and admiration for him or her but just doesn't always show it, and the runner tries to be a little more affirming, your relationship will have a better chance of succeeding.

RUNNING	TENNIS/RACQUETBALL	1

Your relationship can be a difficult one to maintain because you share characteristics that can be destructive to a loving partnership. You're both extremely aggressive and have no qualms about ensuring that all your needs are met. When you both get what you want, there's no problem . . . but beware of the consequences when one of you doesn't get his or her own way! Arguments are likely to be frequent unless you make a special effort to try to keep things calm between you. To manage to do this, the tennis/racquetball playing partner needs to control his or her impulsiveness and avoid saying things that may be hurtful. The high-strung runner needs to work on controlling his or her irritability and insecurity by realizing that the tennis/racquetball player is only human and won't always be as supportive as the runner might like. If both of you try to be a little less selfish, your relationship can prosper.

RUNNING	BALLET/FIGURE SKATING	2

A runner and dancer/skater operate in two totally different spheres. The two of you have little in common and are likely to find that you never fully connect with each other. The runner literally rushes through life, wanting only to reach his or her goals as quickly as possible. In a runner's perspective, getting the job done is of prime importance; enjoying the job as it is performed is seldom a consideration. The dancer, on the other hand, savors the moment and relishes the *process* of doing. Each of your styles will be frustrating to the other partner. The dancer/skater is apt to be annoyed if the runner rushes through lovemaking; the runner re-sents the dancer/skater's tendency to slow down your lives. You may not constantly argue like other pairs, but you won't ever experience a truly close relationship.

BICYCLING BICYCLING	4

There's no question about your compatibility. The two of you are very much alike and feel comfortable with each other. What isn't quite as clear is whether or not your relationship is a healthy one. You're both very traditional and are resistant to change. This can limit your growth, causing you to become stagnant as a couple. You're both acquisitive by nature, a trait that is likely to intensify when paired with another person who is equally into possessions. When two bikers form a union, it's important for them to monitor this characteristic and make sure that they don't get hung up on externals. If you two take care to avoid the pitfalls of a biker-biker coupling, you can have a long and happy relationship.

BICYCLING SWIMMING	3

Profound differences between bikers and swimmers make it difficult for you to understand each other. The biker is apt to feel at loose ends with a swimming partner. Since the biker feels secure only with a large number of possessions, she or he will be uneasy with the swimmer's rejection of these external props. The swimmer is equally likely to be discomfited by the biker's rigid nature and may feel trapped by a partner who never strays far from the established boundaries of his or her life. If the two of you want to stay together, the biker must accept the swimmer's need for freedom and the swimmer will have to respect the biker's desire for a predictable, materialistic life-style.

BICYCLING	WALKING	5

Y ou are a stable couple who are sure to have a calm, comfortable life together. Both of you, as responsible and practical people, are willing to put forth the effort needed to sustain a relationship on a daily basis (as opposed to other pairings, who neglect their problems until they escalate and reach crisis proportions). The only difference between you is that the walker is somewhat more independent than the biker. If the biker can come to terms with the walker's determination to be his or her own person, your relationship should be close to perfect.

BICYCLING	YOGA	3

B ecause the two of you are such different kinds of people, your relationship requires a lot of work to keep it running smoothly. It's easy to lose track of the things that bind you together as a couple if you succumb to the temptation of focusing on your differences. While it can't be denied that you're two separate individuals, each with a unique personal style, there is still that something that drew you together in the first place. The yoga partner is much more cerebral and creative than the down-to-earth biker, but you can still find and capitalize upon your mutual interests. Spend some time trying to recapture the thoughts and feelings you shared when you first became romantically involved; this will enable you to strengthen your emotional ties.

BICYCLING	EXERCISE CLASS	6

Y ou're an enviable couple. There are no major problems that need to be worked out in your relationship. You both like a lot of structure in your lives; living with uncertainty is sure to cause excessive anxiety. Other couples may get bored with this kind of life-style, but it suits both of you. While there's the potential for things to get a little monotonous, the exercise class partner is more outgoing than the biker and will make sure that you enjoy an active social life together. Your network of friendships brings stimulation that would otherwise be missing from your lives.

BICYCLING	MARTIAL ARTS	2

If you're a biking-martial arts couple, expect to experience some trying times. The person who is involved with martial arts is likely to become dissatisfied with the biking partner. Whereas the martial arts practitioner is deeply committed to enhancing his or her personal growth, the biker is perfectly comfortable with the status quo and has no desire to change in any way. This can be frustrating for the martial arts partner, often leading him or her to feel dragged down by the biker. Any attempts by the martial arts partner to alter the biker's life-style is apt to be met by resentment. Therefore, if you're determined to overcome such conflicting natures, you'll need to give each other plenty of breathing space. Be sure to allow sufficient time apart so the martial arts partner can pursue his or her diverse interests without necessitating the biker's involvement (which would be reluctant at best).

BICYCLING	WEIGHT TRAINING	3

The two of you shouldn't have any major problems, but it's unlikely that you'll achieve the same degree of warmth and intimacy that other combinations enjoy. Both the biker and weight trainer are extremely goal-oriented, ensuring that neither of you will stand in the way of the other's achievements. Both of you take a disciplined approach to life, preferring to plan things out rather than let them happen spontaneously. Unfortunately, neither the biker nor weight trainer personalities are expert communicators. You both find it difficult to express emotions and really lay your feelings on the line. Consequently, you may not know each other as well as you could if you were more open with each other.

| BICYCLING | TENNIS/RACQUETBALL | 5 |

You should last a long time as a couple, provided the tennis/racquetball player is careful to control his or her aggressive nature. Although easygoing in temperament, the biker can't be expected to tolerate the hostile behavior that the tennis/racquetball partner shows when frustrated or angry. If the tennis/racquetball player can learn to more appropriately vent his or her negative emotions, the two of you should get along well. The biker is a stabilizing influence, while the tennis/racquetball player brings a dynamic energy and excitement to the relationship. No major difficulties are to be expected since your values and styles, while not identical, don't conflict to any significant extent.

| BICYCLING | BALLET/FIGURE SKATING | 3 |

There will be many times in your relationship when you both question why you're together. There isn't that much that the biker and ballet dancer/figure skater have in common. The dancer/skater's strong communication skills allow him or her to easily express emotions. He or she will very likely be frustrated by the biker's limited abilities in sharing thoughts and feelings. Another potential sore spot is the biker's preference for the familiar versus the dancer/skater's interest in exploring the unknown. The dancer's never ending quest for self-improvement can be unnerving to the biker (who is perfectly satisfied with his current status and feels no need to change in any way). A biker-dancer/skater coupling, if it is to have the best chance of succeeding, requires diligence from both partners. Whereas other pairs can just let their relationship coast, the two of you have to continually monitor how things are going between you. Frequent discussions are a necessity, so you can do your best to stop discord from growing between you.

SWIMMING	SWIMMING	6

A dual swimming couple is bound to have a relationship that's nothing short of fantastic! Each of you individually has a very sensual nature; this trait is even more intensified with a partner who equally enjoys the pleasures of the senses. Life is sure to be erotically fulfilling for you two. Both of you know how to make each moment special and savor it for all it's worth. As one swimmer relating to another, you understand exactly what your partner needs. Your priorities and perspectives are very similar. You both want to enjoy the here and now rather than relentlessly drive yourselves to try to achieve some goal in the distant future. The only negative element that could arise in an otherwise flawless relationship is your shared tendency toward self-indulgence. As two swimming individuals, you each always put your own wants and desires ahead of anyone else's. Making a conscious effort to become a little less selfish could be most beneficial to you as individuals and as a couple.

SWIMMING	WALKING	5

You each have your differences, but you still manage to do well together. The tactually oriented swimmer needs constant hands-on oppportunities to experience the world whereas the visually oriented walker prefers to deal with the occurrences in his or her life on a more abstract and intellectual basis. This essential difference can be beneficial to your relationship as the swimmer brings a sensuality that the walker lacks, and the walker helps the swimmer expand his or her cognitive capabilities. The walker is very serious and responsible; the swimmer is more sybaritic and neglects his or her responsibilities if they're not fun. You can blend these characteristics by letting the walker loosen up and enjoy life more while helping the swimmer develop a more mature attitude toward his or her obligations.

| SWIMMING | YOGA | | 6 |

Count your blessings if you're involved in a swimming-yoga relationship! Your coupling is a nice combination of two gentle personalities. Neither of you is competitive by nature and is therefore able to be fully supportive of your respective partners. Your relationship is relaxed and free of any game-playing. You each bring something special to your union: sensuality (the swimmer) and spirituality (the yoga practitioner). Since the two of you are so ideally suited for each other, there really aren't any potential problems to watch out for. Just be careful never to take your relationship for granted. Nurture it and cherish each other fully to ensure that everything remains wonderful.

| SWIMMING | EXERCISE CLASS | | 2 |

A relationship between a swimmer and exercise class participant is far from an idyllic union. The exercise class partner's goal-oriented energy conflicts with the swimmer's laid-back nature. The swimmer wants to enjoy life in a relaxed manner, taking things as they come and experiencing them as fully as possible, while the exercise class participant is determined to actively pursue his or her ambitions. Another problem is the exercise class partner's authoritative manner. The swimmer can tolerate a great deal before blowing up, but can eventually reach the breaking point when the exercise class partner becomes too bossy and overbearing. This coupling shouldn't be written off as a lost cause, but it does require a commitment on both your parts to compromise and reach some middle ground.

| SWIMMING | MARTIAL ARTS | | 6 |

What a terrific couple the two of you make! Your relationship is blessed with a tranquil harmony since swimmers and martial arts practitioners both like to avoid negative emotions. Both of you will work hard to avoid arguments and can control your anger well. While each of you is individualistic and independent in nature, you manage to merge really well. As a couple you become something greater than the sum of your parts. Your mutual admiration of each other helps to make your relationship special. The swimmer respects the martial arts partner's discipline and strength, while the martial arts practitioner enjoys the swimmer's spontaneity and sensuality. You both should consider yourselves fortunate for finding such ideal partners.

| **SWIMMING** | **WEIGHT TRAINING** | **5** |

When a swimmer and weight trainer become romantically involved, they prove that opposites really do attract. Each of you can complement the other's personality, but you can't expect your partner to become a clone of yourself. While some couples do develop some mutual characteristics, a swimmer and a weight trainer will always be polar opposites. The weight trainer is steadfastly realistic whereas the swimmer is a dreamy idealist. The discipline of the weight trainer markedly contrasts with the swimmer's hedonism. But if you maintain the right perspective, the two of you can respect and enjoy each other. The swimmer can appreciate the way the weight trainer strives to achieve his or her personal goals; the weight trainer can show the swimmer how to savor the moment.

| **SWIMMING** | **TENNIS/RACQUETBALL** | **3** |

When the two of you aren't fighting, you find a great deal of pleasure in each other's company. Unfortunately, arguments are a regular occurrence in your relationship. Most of them are initiated by the tennis/racquetball player because she or he has difficulty accepting the swimmer's laid-back attitude. The tennis/racquetball player does everything quickly and can't understand why the swimmer can't do the same. She or he also is apt to become frustrated about the swimmer's laissez-faire philosophy in which things are just allowed to happen without much energy expended. The tennis/racquetball player is alert to the swimmer's needs and will try to satisfy them, but the swimmer isn't likely to reciprocate and instead primarily looks out for his or her own interests. Since the swimmer will enjoy life regardless of the people in it, the tennis/racquetball player may not feel needed by the aquatic partner. The tennis/racquetball player will need to do some soul searching and self-monitoring to be able to cope with the differences between you two.

| SWIMMING | BALLET/FIGURE SKATING | 6 |

Yours is an interesting, challenging, and ultimately fulfilling relationship. Because both of you possess an intense sensuality and love for beauty, your life together is sure to be filled with a variety of pleasures. In addition to this shared trait, there are some differences between you that are advantageous. The ballet dancer/figure skater has a strong ego and likes a lot of attention and admiration. Fortunately, the swimmer doesn't want to get involved in any power struggles and doesn't mind not being in the limelight. Another beneficial dissimilarity is the ballet dancer/figure skater's discipline as opposed to the swimmer's streak of laziness. Whereas the swimmer is content to just let things go in a relationship, the ballet dancer/figure skater strives for good communication and makes sure you don't deviate from what you want as a couple.

| WALKING | WALKING | 3 |

Surprisingly, two walkers don't necessarily make a compatible couple. Because each of you is a nonconformist and likes to proceed at your own pace, there may be many instances in which you just can't seem to find any common ground. You both may be so busy doing your own things that you never come together as a couple. It is possible for you to live adjacent lives without many problems but not to create a true partnership where you merge your individual styles and needs. If you're willing to have separate lives instead of a shared one, a dual-walking pair can do this in a very efficient manner since you're both practical, steady, and dependable.

WALKING	YOGA	5

Neither identical twins nor total opposites, a walker and yoga devotee are quite compatible in most respects. Both of you are introspective and intellectual, although in differing degrees. The walker manages to relate to the outside world far more than the yoga partner. This may initially unnerve the yoga partner because she or he is most comfortable with limited contact with the external environment, but will gradually become more acclimated to it and realize that it yields a more balanced life-style which is ultimately more healthy. Since you both insist on being true to yourselves, your relationship is filled with integrity and honesty. Neither of you is competitive, so you're able to work together to help each other reach your individual potential.

WALKING	EXERCISE CLASS	2

Proceed with caution in this relationship. You'll have some difficulty understanding each other and accepting your differences. The exercise class partner is very much a conformist, whereas the walker is an individualist who ignores social procedures and trends. The walker will be disdainful of the exercise class partner's constant need to keep up with and copy other people; the exercise class partner will be embarrassed that the walker is so different from the rest of his or her friends. What you both need to recognize is that you have some traits in common. You share a need for structure in your lives and need a set routine to be comfortable. If you can learn to emphasize your similarities and respect each other's differences, you'll find happiness together.

WALKING	MARTIAL ARTS	6

The two of you were made for each other. You share the same independent and practical natures. You both know how you want to live and aren't willing to live by someone else's standards. Neither one of you is interested in pretending to be something you're not. You can be real with each other and know that you'll be accepted. The walker does have a tendency to get into a rut where everything becomes very predictable, but the martial arts partner can gently expose him or her to new experiences and challenges. Your even temperaments enable you to avoid the bitter arguments other couples experience. This relationship should be great for both of you.

WALKING	WEIGHT TRAINING	4

You'll have some problems in this pairing, but it's possible to make a go of it if the walker makes some changes. Both of you are assertive and independent. You'll each stand up for what you want and won't allow anyone else to take advantage of you. The troubles occur when one of you wants something extremely different from what the other wants. This can happen frequently because your needs are not at all similar. The walker is more laid-back and prefers to live in a down-to-earth, predictable way whereas the weight trainer can be happy only when conquering new vistas. The weight trainer's continual striving for glory and recognition can be tiresome to the walker (who is more apt to live his or her life without much fanfare). Your relationship can succeed only if the walker gratifies the weight trainer's ego by providing frequent positive strokes without getting any in return. The walker will also need to become more comfortable with the unfamiliar as she or he accompanies the weight lifting partner on new adventures.

WALKING	TENNIS/RACQUETBALL	1

There's no getting around the substantial differences between you. The tennis/racquetball player is aggressive; the walker is quite passive. The placid walker is very much in control of his or her emotions, but the tennis/racquetball player is likely to experience erratic mood swings. The tennis/racquetball player enjoys spontaneity while the walker favors a carefully planned and organized life-style. You can't downplay these differences since they are significant, but you can try to help each other strive toward more of a happy medium. Instead of one of you being the aggressor and the other the passive bystander, both of you should work toward becoming assertive. Rather than the walker keeping such a tight rein on his or her emotions and the tennis/racquetball player being highly emotional, the two of you need to develop the ability to express your emotions calmly. These measures will prove to be very helpful for your relationship.

WALKING	BALLET/FIGURE SKATING	3

A walker and a dancer/skater aren't exactly wrong together, but you'll have some challenges to overcome. You're quite different and can't expect to connect on a very deep level. The dancer/figure skater's lively, expressive style is nothing at all like the walker's more subdued and introverted nature. The walker has difficulty understanding the dancer/figure skater's need for recognition and attention since the walker is most comfortable being alone and going through life quietly. Still another difference is that the walker seeks a well-balanced, practical life-style whereas the dancer/figure skater will neglect some parts of his or her life if they're not appealing or meaningful (a trait that filters out what isn't pleasurable to the dancer/skater but can prevent him or her from being a dependable partner to share a life with). Only the two of you can decide if there's enough that's right with your relationship to make the compromises you'll need to be happy.

| YOGA   YOGA | 6 |

The two of you have the type of relationship other couples can only dream about. You're patient and supportive with each other. Your life goals are usually quite similar, but even when they're not, you both can accept your partner's needs. The deep spirituality that you share helps you to focus on the important things in life, enabling you to seek and find meaning in your activities and thoughts. Caring about each other comes naturally; you don't need to devote a lot of effort to maintaining your wonderful relationship. Your happiness is sure to last forever.

| YOGA   EXERCISE CLASS | 3 |

Be prepared for major turbulence in this relationship! Because you're so different from each other, you'll have to work hard to find some common ground. The yoga partner is more patient and open-minded than any other type of exerciser, but may find it difficult to deal with some of the characteristics of the exercise class partner. The exercise class participant's boundless energy and competitiveness is completely foreign to the yoga partner's nature. On the other hand, the exercise class partner doesn't understand the yoga partner's serenity and introspection. But you both have the needed discipline to make your union work. Mutual respect and caring can go a long way in making a successful relationship. The exercise class partner can reap some benefit from the yoga partner's tranquillity, while the yoga partner can profit from the exerciser's assertiveness, organizational ability, and competence in the everyday world.

| YOGA   MARTIAL ARTS | 6 |

A relationship that combines a partner who practices yoga with one who performs martial arts is bound to be a winner!

There are some small differences between the two of you, but you're very similar when it comes to the important things in life. Because both of you want to grow as individuals, you each can help the other realize his or her full potential. There's a mutual admiration: for the quiet inner strength of the yoga partner and for the confidence and practicality of the martial arts partner. Your relationship is sure to endure on a permanent basis.

YOGA	WEIGHT TRAINING	2

Your relationship is not totally incompatible, but you can expect to have a lot of misunderstandings. Both of you are resourceful, determined individuals with a strong orientation to reaching your goals; the problem is that your goals and, especially, your methods of achieving them differ so radically. The yoga partner may be resentful of the martial arts partner's assertiveness, often finding that his or her own needs go unsatisfied. The yoga partner may also have difficulty accepting the weight trainer's narcissism, preferring a more austere attitude. On the other hand, the weight trainer may not be able to relate to the yoga partner's tendency to downplay emotions. The two of you will have to make sure to always maintain good communication, which enables you to talk over your differences and resolve conflicts. Becoming careless and allowing communication to falter will lead to a speedy ending of your relationship.

YOGA	TENNIS/RACQUETBALL	1

It should come as no surprise to either of you that you're extremely different in temperaments, interests, and values. The tennis/racquetball player would be happy socializing all the time, whereas the yoga partner thinks that true quality time is spent alone or with one very close companion. The steady, controlled, slow-to-burn yoga partner may be unnerved by the tennis/racquetball player's volatile temper. The tennis/racquetball player's extreme competitiveness is at odds with the yoga partner's noncompetitive, inner-directed philosophy. It would be highly beneficial for you each to try to absorb some of the other person's strengths (while, of course, still retaining your unique individuality). The yoga partner will eventually begin to participate a little more in the external world without always escaping from it, and the tennis/racquetball partner may stop trying to constantly prove him- or herself and ultimately enjoy life more.

YOGA	BALLET/FIGURE SKATING	6

The two of you share common traits, but there are enough dissimilarities to keep things interesting. Your relationship should work well. The dancer wants to be the center of attention, but this doesn't present a problem because the yoga partner doesn't mind taking a backseat and letting the dancer/skater be in the limelight. Neither of you is satisfied by material goals; you both strive for higher purposes and achievements. The yoga partner is somewhat more spiritual than the dancer/skater, but the dancer/skater is more expressive and communicative. You both are comfortable with your individual selves. You know who you are and you're secure in that knowledge. Your life together should be joyous and fulfilling.

EXERCISE CLASS	EXERCISE CLASS	4

You may be birds of the same feather, but that doesn't mean that your nest will always be filled with domestic bliss. Both of you are very gregarious and want to be surrounded by lots of other people. This ensures a terrific social life, but there can be conflicts when you don't like the same people. You're both also very competitive. What one of you gets, the other wants. You would both like to be leaders and hate to compromise. However, it *is* possible for you to learn to coexist in a harmonious manner. Both of you have the discipline and energy to make your relationship work. Arrange to spend one night at home with just each other every week to discuss your lives and your future plans. Be sure to keep an open mind about your partner's needs and desires so that you can plan your strategy for functioning together as a united couple.

EXERCISE CLASS	MARTIAL ARTS	5

Yours is a winning combination. There are some differences between you, but things balance out so that you function as an evenly matched pair. Each of you respects the other for his or her abilities, whether it's the strength and practicality of the martial arts partner or the energy and determination of the exercise class partner. Because both of you know how to work through negative emotions, you generally are able to avoid the arguments that plague other couples. The only potential problem is that the martial arts partner is extremely independent, whereas the more social exercise class partner likes to rely on others for support. If the martial arts partner begins to feel smothered by the exerciser's need for companionship and constant stroking, the exerciser should be encouraged to partially fulfill these needs through other people. The exerciser has enough social resources not to have to rely exclusively on the martial arts partner to satisfy his or her needs.

EXERCISE CLASS	WEIGHT TRAINING	5

The two of you make a dynamic pair. You can achieve whatever goals you set for yourselves as individuals and as a couple. You're both competitive but have enough respect for each other so that you're supportive of the other's ambitions. There can be the danger of too much striving and overreaching as you encourage each other toward new achievements and continually test your abilities. It is quite possible for one or both of you to become overly stressed and then for your relationship to suffer as a result. Since relaxation doesn't come naturally to either of you, you need to consciously devote some quiet time to just being together without trying to achieve anything.

EXERCISE CLASS	TENNIS/RACQUETBALL	4

It's no wonder you're a popular couple. Both of you are bright, energetic, outgoing individuals. Do be aware, though, that all your activity may prevent you from really connecting and forming a real union. You could easily find yourselves leading adjacent lives that never intersect in any meaningful way. You both also need to watch out for your aggressive tendencies (and this goes double for the tennis/racquetball player). Unchecked aggression that isn't put to constructive use can be destructive to your relationship. However, with some insight and empathy, you can learn to be kind and caring to each other. It's inevitable that you'll always have a few kinks to work out of this pairing, but there definitely will be more positives than negatives overall.

EXERCISE CLASS	BALLET/FIGURE SKATING	5

Although your temperaments are quite different, you can have a happy coupling. The ballet dancer/figure skater's strong ego isn't a problem for the exerciser. If the dancer/skater wants to have star billing in the relationship, the exercise class partner is perfectly happy to let those needs be fulfilled. It's not that the exerciser isn't competitive; it's just that he or she is more interested in self-competition by trying to reach his or her own potential. The dancer/skater can understand this striving to do one's best and won't interfere with the exercise partner's quest. Other couples may have better communication and more warmth in their relationships, but the two of you are bound to be a productive pair who experience growth and achievement in all facets of your lives.

MARTIAL ARTS	MARTIAL ARTS	6

Some people might wonder how you two get along so well since you're both such strong individuals. But your relationship *does* work, and it doesn't require one partner to be the leader and the other to be the more submissive follower. You're both comfortable with power and strength, but neither of you abuses it. You're happy functioning as equal partners. Each of you has an independent streak, but you also take great pleasure in each other's companionship. Together the two of you can have it all . . . dynamic careers, exciting leisure time, satisfying social lives, and an enviable love life.

| MARTIAL ARTS | WEIGHT TRAINING | 5 |

For the most part, you're a well-matched couple. Both of you are disciplined, assertive when you need to be, interested in new challenges and in developing yourselves to your greatest potential. Some power struggles may be unavoidable since you both want to be strong and authoritative. It will be necessary to carefully monitor the trouble spots in your relationship so that you can discover and deal with the issues that threaten to break up an otherwise happy union. Allow each of you to be in charge of certain areas of your life together, ensuring that both will have a voice in the partnership. Emphasize areas of mutual interest so that you can work in unison to create the type of life you both want.

| MARTIAL ARTS | TENNIS/RACQUETBALL | 5 |

Yours should be a fairly successful pairing. Both of you are dynamic and independent people. You're willing to expend the needed effort to obtain what you want. You can be supportive of each other's dreams and ambitions. There may be some friction at times because of the tennis/racquetball player's unchanneled aggressiveness and impatience, but the martial arts partner is usually able to diffuse this and focus instead on the love and commitment you have for each other. If the two of you remain determined to maintain your relationship even when things occasionally get rocky, there is little doubt that you'll be together on a long-term basis.

MARTIAL ARTS	BALLET/FIGURE SKATING	6

You are highly compatible. You both know your individual selves well and are secure in that knowledge, but neither of you is content to rest on your laurels. Opportunities for personal growth and exploration are a necessity in your lives. Both of you want to reach your fullest potential and wouldn't dream of interfering with each other's self-development. The martial arts partner is sometimes too introspective for his or her own good, but the dancer/skater's more outgoing nature and excellent communication skills can help counteract this tendency. Whereas other individuals may have difficulty dealing with the dancer/skater's ego, the martial arts partner is able to rise above it and refrain from trying to compete. This tolerance for the dancer/skater's vanity goes a long way in preventing arguments between the two of you. When you occasionally do fight, the martial arts partner's rationality and sense of fair play enables the two of you to work things out in a loving manner.

WEIGHT TRAINING	WEIGHT TRAINING	5

Other couples might enjoy a quieter, gentler relationship, but your shared style works for *you*. There's nothing timid in the way you relate to each other. Both of you are extremely assertive and never hesitate to go after the goals you set. You're forthright in telling your respective partners what you need from the relationship. If you sometimes step on each other's toes on the way to getting what you want, you're thick-skinned enough to not let it bother you. You can both be quite narcissistic, but your mutual admiration ensures that you won't get overly self-involved. Since you're both highly disciplined, you're able to achieve your ambitions as a couple.

WEIGHT TRAINING	TENNIS/RACQUETBALL	6

In most respects you should enjoy a congenial relationship. You're both active, committed people who become thoroughly involved in everything you do. You do things in an all-or-nothing way, so once you decide on a life partner, you throw all your energies into the relationship. Because neither of you gets discouraged easily, you won't give up on each other even if you experience some problems. You both are goal-oriented and have a strong drive for success. The tennis/racquetball player is most concerned with achievement in the business world, while the weight trainer is more focused on intrapersonal challenges (such as avocational interests or mental and physical fitness). Thus you're able to complement each other in a way that assures that you'll have a full, abundant, whole life together.

WEIGHT TRAINING	BALLET/FIGURE SKATING	3

Your relationship requires constant maintenance and sometimes even first aid to keep it functioning. The two of you are alike in several ways, but this often is detrimental to your ability to fully care for each other. You both have strong egos and tend to be self-centered. Neither of you is willing to make even a small sacrifice for the sake of your respective partners. When you both want the same thing, you make a dynamic duo who work well together. But when your desires are different (as is often the case when one partner is into ballet/skating and the other is a weight trainer), each of you can be ruthless in trying to obtain what you want, often to the point of becoming adversaries. This relationship can succeed only if you can learn to fight fairly and to take the other person's feelings into account.

| TENNIS/RACQUETBALL | TENNIS/RACQUETBALL | 2 |

You're exactly alike, but this similarity can be dangerous for your relationship. Both of you are extremely high-strung and aggressive. You would have this temperament with any type of partner you had, but another tennis/racquetball player intensifies these traits even more. You're both extremely competitive and wouldn't ever allow your respective partners to get an edge on you. Both of you want to be the winner in everything you do, individually and as a couple. This can be positive in some ways since you challenge each other to strive for excellence, but it becomes counterproductive if you lose your ability to help and be supportive of each other. Your mutual impatience can lead to short tempers and frequent arguments. You'll both need to make an extra effort in exhibiting the patience necessary to be happy together.

| TENNIS/RACQUETBALL | BALLET/FIGURE SKATING | 6 |

Yours is a lively relationship, full of surprises and challenges. The tennis/racquetball partner's spontaneity nicely complements the dancer/skater's more controlled nature. While the tennis/racquetball player keeps the dancer/skater guessing as to what she or he will do next, the dancer/skater helps to keep the tennis/racquetball player from becoming too impulsive and doing anything rash. The tennis/racquetball player is often aggressive and domineering, but this isn't a problem for the dancer/skater, who has a quiet strength and can more than hold his or her own with anyone else. Since the tennis/racquetball player has a tendency to become overly focused on one specific area of his or her life, the multifaceted personality of the dancer/skater can help to maintain a more well-balanced life-style. Each of you finds a satisfying partner in the other.

BALLET/FIGURE SKATING   **BALLET/FIGURE SKATING**   1

Unless the two of you can learn to curb your egos, you will have a very trying relationship. The problem is the burning desire of most dancers for attention and admiration. A dancer is not well equipped to provide anyone else with the needed strokes since he or she is too busy seeking it for him- or herself. So when two dancers are romantically involved, they both experience the frustration of not getting what they need from their respective partners. As resentment builds and competition for the spotlight grows, you each may resort to negative tactics that can destroy your relationship. Both of you have a lot to offer (e.g., a well-developed sense of beauty, a sensual nature, and good communication skills), but you will both have to work to put your egos aside to enjoy life together.

8

Pets

Some psychological researchers believe that the kind of pet you own says something about your personality. Someone who chooses to own a cat, for instance, has different character traits from a dog owner. Therefore, your compatibility as a couple can be revealed by the type of pet you each prefer.

To locate your compatibility profile, just pair your individual pet preferences. Keep in mind that the type of pet you like best may not be the pet you own now (or have owned in the past). For example, you may have inherited a cat when you're really much more of a dog-lover, or you may have settled for fish because your physician warned you that birds could aggravate your allergies. Choose the pet you'd most like to have if you were allowed only one pet but had no other restrictions (such as your partner's preferences, space, time, allergies, etc.) Note that the rodent category includes mice, hamsters, ferrets, guinea pigs, and so on, while the "other" classification includes every other type of animal (e.g., snakes, lizards, llamas, monkeys, or kangaroos).

Person 1	Pet	Person 2
_____	Cat	_____
_____	Dog	_____
_____	Bird	_____
_____	Fish	_____
_____	Turtle	_____
_____	Rodent	_____
_____	Other	_____

Now compare your answers and read your compatibility profile.

CAT CAT	4

The two of you will be sure to give each other plenty of breathing space. It's not that you don't care; you both just have many of your own interests and are highly independent by nature. Make a concerted effort to regularly connect with each other and spend some time together so you don't end up leading totally separate lives, becoming more like strangers than lovers.

CAT DOG	3

Your relationship has a fifty-fifty chance of working. You can complement each other and add some qualities the other person is missing (the dog owner adds an affectionate note; the cat owner helps the dog owner become more self-reliant and capable), or you can fight constantly because you're so different. A lot depends on the dog owner. The cat owner's nature and behavior is fairly consistent, but the dog owner's temperament can experience some wide fluctuations ranging from friendly and passive to hostile and aggressive. If the dog owner can control these negative impulses, the outlook for the two of you should be fairly good.

CAT BIRD	2

The major problem in your relationship is your differing needs for companionship. The bird owner is highly sociable and desires a lot of togetherness. The cat owner doesn't want this since it is contrary to his or her independent nature; he or she may therefore feel smothered by the bird's demands for conversation and closeness. This relationship can work only if the bird can find other social outlets for those times when the cat wants to be alone.

CAT FISH	2

Although the cat owner doesn't want to be bothered with a demanding or needy partner, she or he still wants someone who's more committed to the relationship than the fish owner. It's true that the cat and fish share a desire for a stimulating and active life. But the cat also needs a partner with a lot of emotional warmth (to make up for the cat's own lack of this quality). The fish never really relates to the cat in an affectionate way, leading the cat to feel vaguely dissatisfied with the relationship. For this relationship to be a happy one, both partners—but especially the fish—have to make an effort to be more affectionate.

CAT	TURTLE	2

While you won't experience the frequent fights other couples endure, you'll find that you don't have much of a relationship. The cat will not be happy with the turtle's cautious nature, feeling that the turtle slows him or her down. The turtle owner in turn often feels overwhelmed by the cat owner's active pursuit of challenge and adventure, since a more routine, placid approach is favored by the turtle. Unless you make an effort to compromise your desires, you'll most likely end up spending as little time together as possible.

CAT	RODENT	6

You'll lead a wonderfully full life together. You won't make heavy demands on each other; instead, you'll strive to get the most out of life as individuals and as a couple. Neither of you is a couch potato. You both enjoy exploring the world and all it has to offer. Together you can have the action-packed, stimulating life you each relish.

CAT	OTHER	4

The owner of another type of pet can be an intriguing partner for the cat. The cat enjoys novelty and adventure as much as the other-pet owner. This bold spirit that you share can result in an exciting life for you as a couple. However, there are some differences between you that will need to be addressed from time to time. Although the cat is independent by nature, she or he still wants a caring, demonstrative partner. The other-pet owner finds it difficult to be affectionate. The cat will either have to learn to accept this trait and capitalize upon the positive aspects of the relationship or find another partner.

| DOG | DOG | 4 |

Most of the time you'll have a warm, loving relationship. You'll generally be mutually supportive of each other's dreams and desires, doing everything possible to make them a reality. But there can be a destructive element that creeps into your relationship. Moodiness can be intense in a dual-dog pairing, and when you find yourself at odds, you both are prone to harboring your resentment and then overreacting. But if you try to minimize such situations, you should be very happy together.

| DOG | BIRD | 6 |

The two of you have a high degree of compatibility. The bird owner isn't interested in any power plays, but will be more than willing to let the dog owner be the leader. All the bird wants is a happy homelife with an amiable partner. The dog will be happy to provide this companionship because he or she appreciates the pleasantness that the bird brings into his or her life.

| DOG | FISH | 1 |

The two of you can easily misunderstand each other. The dog owner may view the fish owner's aloof nature as being uncaring and selfish. In turn, the fish is likely to perceive the affectionate dog as making too many demands on the fish's time and attention. Communication is essential for your relationship to work. By talking over your feelings and discussing your concerns, the dog will learn that the fish, although reserved and undemonstrative at times, does care. The fish can also let it be known when the dog is becoming too clinging and possessive.

DOG	TURTLE	6

You complement each other perfectly. The dog owner appreciates the steadiness of the turtle owner, finding him or her to be a partner who can really be counted on. The turtle's emotional stability serves as an excellent counterbalance to the dog's mood swings. But this is not a one-sided relationship; the turtle benefits from the dog's fearlessness, thus helping the turtle to become less withdrawn and more actively involved in life. Yours is a case where opposites really do attract.

DOG	RODENT	5

Although you don't always have a lot in common, you still manage to respect each other. You can have a good life together, filled with interesting activities. The rodent enjoys being on the go and this keeps the dog from becoming too sedentary. Conversely, the dog prevents the rodent from engaging in constant activity that often becomes unfocused and meaningless. Thus, by helping each other, you both can lead balanced and satisfying lives.

DOG	OTHER	2

Your relationship may have its share of troubles. While the dog owner is self-confident enough not to be threatened by the other pet owner's craving for excitement, she or he will still want a great deal of closeness. But the other pet owner often wants to pursue adventure without being tied down. These problems don't have to be insurmountable, however. If you make sure that the dog has an active network of friends and family to provide the emotional support that is not always available from the other pet owner, you both can feel fulfilled.

BIRD BIRD	4

Yours is a fun pairing. Because you're both so gregarious and love to carry on a conversation, you'll provide each other with a lot of social and intellectual stimulation. Neither of you is a worrier; you each tend to see the bright side of everything. Consequently, there won't be much moodiness in your relationship. There are, however, two things you need to watch out for. First, make sure to be good listeners for each other by avoiding the temptation to constantly verbalize without hearing what your partner is saying. In addition, try to make sure you don't become all talk and no action. Stop discussing and start doing!

BIRD FISH	2

Each of you has needs the other can't easily fill. The fish owner wants total freedom without any restrictions so that she or he can have an active and pleasurable life-style. But the bird owner desires the security of a stable, predictable way of life. Demands by the bird for companionship make the fish feel tied down, while the bird becomes resentful of the fish's disinterest in spending quality time together. You'll have to work extra hard at communication and compromise if your relationship is to last.

BIRD TURTLE	5

Neither of you is passionate or even very demonstrative by nature, but that doesn't preclude you from having a very satisfactory relationship with each other. The bird owner will be the more giving partner on an emotional level, but the turtle owner can bring some special elements of his or her own. The turtle can help the bird become more focused rather than scatter his or her energies among many projects and never really finish any of them. Because you appreciate each other for unique characteristics (the bird's communicative abilities and positive outlook, the turtle's steadiness and determination), your relationship will be supportive and caring.

BIRD   RODENT   6

No problems in your relationship! You're ideally suited for each other. Both of you are extremely active and alert. You know how to enjoy yourselves; you're skilled at filling every minute with fun activities. But the rodent owner isn't just a hedonist. He or she isn't afraid of hard work and will determinedly do whatever it takes to reach his or her goals. This trait makes the rodent an excellent partner for the less ambitious bird owner and prevents the bird from living a life that is pleasurable but ultimately purposeless.

BIRD   OTHER   1

There are several conflicts in your relationship. The major one is your differing perspectives on stability. The bird owner can be happy only when involved in a long-term relationship that provides complete security. But the other-pet owner feels stifled by predictability and may avoid commitment to just one partner. Another problem is that the bird is highly verbal while the other-pet owner is more of a doer than a talker. The bird's continuous chatter can be annoying to the other-pet owner, just as the other-pet owner's reticence can be frustrating to the bird owner. To prevent these problems from escalating to the point of no return, the bird needs to allow the other-pet owner sufficient freedom for experimentation and adventure. Because the other-pet owner will never be much of a communicator, the bird needs to make sure that she or he has a number of friends to confide in and chat with.

FISH FISH	5

While you won't be as loving and supportive as other pairings, you can lead a life together that suits you both well. You each know exactly what you want and feel no shame about pursuing what you desire. You're into satisfying your individual needs before those of a partner, but fortunately you share the same sensuality and love of pleasure. You both take as effortless an approach to life as possible; hard work doesn't appeal to either of you. You're much more interested in enjoying yourselves than in trying to reach some material goal. A double-fish life-style is not for everyone, but the two of you will enjoy every moment you have together.

FISH TURTLE	6

Your differences are likely complementary, making for a successful union. The turtle owner will be the responsible partner in your relationship. She or he is perfectly happy taking care of the little details of your lives and making sure that all the work gets done. The fish owner can't be counted on to be as productive as the turtle, but he or she will make life more pleasurable. Without the sensual and fun-loving fish, the turtle won't experience much joy in living; with a fish for a partner, the turtle can achieve a rewarding balance between work and play, duty and delight.

FISH RODENT	6

You're enough alike to be compatible, but you also have enough dissimilarities to keep things interesting. Your life together will be very full since you both like stimulating activities and hate being bored. The fish owner brings a sensuous element to the relationship, showing the rodent owner how to take pleasure in daily life instead of simply having a hectic life-style that is busy but not always satisfying. The rodent can help the fish learn to achieve a more purposeful approach to daily living, still affording enjoyment while not being so hedonistic to the exclusion of everything else. When a fish and rodent join forces, you'll have fun but will accomplish other more serious goals as well.

FISH   OTHER   **5**

Neither one of you wants a needy partner; you both know what you want out of life and don't want someone holding you down while you try to get it. Other relationships can be warmer, closer, and more romantic than yours. But you'll both be happy together. You want to be free to live your own lives without worrying about anyone else. Some people would say you're self-centered, but you don't care because you don't need their approval. Instead, you'll pursue your individual interests and will only occasionally come together when these interests coincide. You both like stimulating experiences (the other-pet owner especially likes to be involved in trying new things), so it is possible for you to spend some quality time together in your quest for adventure and pleasure.

TURTLE   TURTLE   **6**

Some relationships are exciting, but yours isn't one of them. This doesn't bother either of you in the least. In fact, you'd both be unnerved by a partner who has unpredictable mood swings and wild ideas. You're much more comfortable with someone similar in temperament to your own, and you each fill that bill for the other. You share the same quiet determination to do what needs to be done. You also have a mutual preference for living in a predictable, orderly way. Steadiness and loyalty are the qualities you both want in a partner, and they're what you each get in a double-turtle relationship.

TURTLE	RODENT	3

Y ou'll have difficulty in working together to achieve the goals you set for yourselves. You're both ambitious, but in entirely different ways. The turtle owner is extremely methodical and likes to approach everything in a step-by-step manner, completely finishing what she or he has started before moving on to the next thing. The rodent owner lacks the turtle's patience and has a tendency to rush haphazardly through life, frantically engaged in a range of activities. Although you need to avoid participating together in demanding projects (e.g., remodeling a house) because you'll have major disagreements, you both are even-tempered enough to make your relationship work in almost every other aspect of your lives.

TURTLE	OTHER	1

The two of you have highly different perspectives on commitment. The other-pet owner is a novelty seeker who easily gets bored and likes the idea of periodically changing partners, but the turtle owner desperately wants a partner for a lifetime. You also feel different about stability in general. Change is not something to which the turtle easily adapts, whereas the other-pet owner thrives on it.

But if you care about each other, you'll need to try to merge your viewpoints. The turtle needs to become more amenable to variety and new experiences in your shared life so that the other-pet owner doesn't become bored and unchallenged. In return, the other-pet owner must respect the turtle's need for commitment and make every effort to reassure the turtle that she or he is ready to settle down for the long term.

| RODENT   RODENT | 5 |

You're a high-energy couple who make other couples seem lazy by comparison. You'll always be on the go. While you won't have many deep conversations with each other, you'll still feel close because you share so many challenging activities together. Just remember that even people with your energy levels can burn out, so be sure to set aside some time to recharge. Learn to relax together and also to set some limits for yourselves. It's impossible for even a double-rodent couple to keep going at your typical frantic pace without ever taking a break. If either of you suddenly crashes from an overload in your lives, it will obviously impact upon your relationship in a negative way . . . so try to develop a more balanced life-style.

| RODENT   OTHER | 4 |

Although there may be frequent clashes in your dealings with each other, you'll still manage to enjoy your relationship. You both like to be challenged through involvement in activities that absorb your interest because they're either unique or demanding. Neither of you is comfortable with overt sentimentality; you prefer the implicit recognition that you're together because you want to be and you feel that's enough. But you both can be opinionated and outspoken. This becomes a problem when you want different things and insist that the other person share your point of view. Because you're both such strong personalities, there's little that can be done to remedy this situation. All you can do is accept the unavoidable bickering and make the most of the positives in your relationship.

OTHER   OTHER   **3**

A double other-pet owning couple does not usually have a very stable relationship. You're both too impetuous and impulsive to want to stick it out when things get rough. Because you share a low tolerance for boredom, you find yourselves yearning for the excitement of getting to know a new partner after you've been with someone for a while. But it would be beneficial for you both to fight this tendency to continually escape into new relationships. A different partner will be stimulating at first but will, of course, eventually become just as familiar and routine as your old one. If you resolve to keep things exciting between the two of you without resorting to running off to someone new, you'll enjoy each other for a lifetime.

9

Decorating Style

Unless you've inherited your entire home furnishings or you've been financially unable to decorate as you want, your home probably reflects a preference for one of the five major decorating styles: modern, traditional, Oriental, English country, or American country. The style you choose is no accident; it's based on an emotional response to the look and feeling of a particular style. This identification with a certain style begins to form early in life and can change over time. Since a preference for one style over another reveals a great deal about your personality, a couple's compatibility can be analyzed by the style each partner favors.

After reading the following descriptions of the five styles, each of you should choose the one style you find most appealing. Then combine your decorating styles to learn whether the personal styles they reflect blend harmoniously or irrevocably clash.

Modern: Includes Scandinavian furniture; teakwood; high tech; metals; chrome and glass; laminated furniture; soft, unstructured, cushiony chairs and sofas; earth tones such as browns, desert beiges, and pinks; bright prints.

Traditional: Includes antiques; satins, brocades, and tweeds; muted colors; heavy wooden furniture, particularly in walnut and cherry; early American furnishings; accessories that are both functional and decorative.

Oriental: Includes lacquered furniture; painted screens; rattan or bamboo; red and black accents; bright silks; painted screens; Japanese/Chinese artifacts.

English country: Includes bright floral chintz; overstuffed sofas and armchairs; needlepoint; paintings of hunting scenes; old portraits; many floral arrangements; lots of collectibles and books.

American country: Includes oak and bleached pine furniture; homemade objects; quilts; rocking chairs; calico curtains; animal motifs such as ducks, pigs, cows; daisy or seashell designs.

Person 1	Decorating style	Person 2
_____	Modern	_____
_____	Traditional	_____
_____	Oriental	_____
_____	English country	_____
_____	American country	_____

MODERN   MODERN   **4**

Your life together is sure to be exciting because you're both open to trying new things. Neither of you is afraid to experiment with the unknown. Your relationship will never become stagnant since it is subjected to ever-changing outside influences. Your friends, the clothes you wear, the foods you eat, the music you listen to, can all be drastically different from one year to the next. While your philosophies of life and ultimate goals may differ, one thing remains constant: the sophistication you bring to everything you do. On the down side, neither one of you is very affectionate by nature nor are you as sentimental as other couples. It is easy for you to feel emotionally detached from each other. Do try to set aside some time from your busy lives to become regularly reacquainted and to show how much you each care about the other.

MODERN TRADITIONAL	1

You're not anything alike. The traditionalist feels comfortable only in familiar surroundings with familiar people, whereas the modernist always craves new experiences. The modernist is intrigued by the future; the traditionalist is firmly rooted in the past. Family is extremely important to the traditionalist and relatively insignificant to the modernist. You'll have to make an extra effort to blend your unique identities into a successful partnership. The modernist will need to strive to provide the reassurance and commitment that the traditionalist needs. Conversely, the traditionalist will have to become more open to changes so that the innovative and creative modernist feels challenged.

MODERN ORIENTAL	4

Both of you are sophisticated individuals who want more out of life than mere survival. You both want to experience a more satisfying life-style than the mundane existence that so many people find themselves trapped in. But your definitions of happiness in life are quite different. The modernist wants to live in an easy but elegant and exciting manner, whereas the Orientalist seeks a simple, balanced life-style filled with quiet grace and serenity. It is very likely that the Orientalist, who is always searching for the truly important things in life, will find the modernist shallow and materialistic. In many instances you'll find yourselves unable to agree on even the most basic issues. What appeals to one partner will seldom appeal to the other. But if you can learn to compromise and integrate your two styles, your relationship can be something quite special.

| MODERN | ENGLISH COUNTRY | 2 |

Growing apart would be easy for the two of you to do because you're so different. The English country partner has a warm interest in people that is totally foreign to the modernist. The partner who favors English country loves to stay at home for intimate conversation with a small group of special friends, whereas the modernist finds such sedate activity to be boring and prefers instead to be out and about, enjoying the stimulation of large numbers of people. To counteract the tendency to drift away from each other, you'll each need to make some changes. The modernist must become more communicative and caring, while the English country partner tries to be a little more open to spontaneity and variety. As for your social lives, the English country partner will need to expand his or her horizons by mingling with relatively unfamiliar people as the modernist works on developing deeper friendships with just a few. Such compromises will greatly improve your compatibility.

| MODERN | AMERICAN COUNTRY | 1 |

Because you have almost nothing in common, it's necessary for the two of you to devote significant time and energy trying to understand each other. Without an atmosphere of mutual tolerance and respect, the modernist is likely to view the American country partner's innocence as a lack of sophistication. The image-conscious modernist may be annoyed by the American country partner's lack of artifice and social polish. Without sufficient communication, the American country partner will see the modernist as pretentious, cold, and uncaring. Make a serious commitment right now to expend the effort to know and appreciate each other so that your relationship can survive and prosper.

TRADITIONAL TRADITIONAL	5

A loving, secure partnership is virtually guaranteed when both partners are traditionalists. You're extremely loyal to each other and won't give up on your relationship even during tough times. You both care deeply about rituals and traditions; both of you want to stick with the tried and true. There is no question that you're more comfortable with each other than you could ever be with other partners. But it is also an unfortunate fact that being together will accentuate your reluctance to ever take any chances or to experiment with the unknown. Your mutual preference to play it safe can prevent you from growing as individuals and as a couple. If you're both satisfied with your lives and don't want to make any changes, there won't be a problem. But if one of you should decide that you've become too stagnant, you may need to seek the help of a trusted adviser who can show you some strategies for breaking out of your rut.

TRADITIONAL ORIENTAL	4

The two of you generally are a good pairing. Both the traditionalist and the Orientalist personalities seek a sense of peaceful contentment in their lives. Neither one is interested in trying to impress other people; you both know who you are and would never try to be something else. Each of you respects tradition, but the Orientalist also enjoys experimenting with the unknown and can broaden the traditionalist's horizons. There shouldn't be any major hazards in your relationship unless the traditionalist becomes overly involved in materialistic pursuits. The spiritually inclined Orientalist may have difficulty with the traditionalist partner's need to accumulate a lot of possessions. If you can learn to unconditionally accept each other's styles, you should have a fulfilling life together.

| TRADITIONAL | ENGLISH COUNTRY | 6 |

You'll enjoy a calm, predictable life with each other. You both are into family and friends. Roots are important to both traditionalists and English country devotees. Each of you feels secure when you adhere to familiar customs and routines in your lives. Other couples might find this structure confining, but it works for you two. People who don't know you well may think you're somewhat formal, but that's only your public personae. In the privacy of your own home you both are relaxed, fun-loving, and sociable. The combination of traditionalist and English country personalities ensures complete compatibility. It's highly unlikely that you'll experience any problems in this relationship.

| TRADITIONAL | AMERICAN COUNTRY | 6 |

You can expect your relationship to be a happy one. You share the same values and life goals. Because both of you care deeply about people, you're able to readily express your affection for each other. The two of you believe in a lifelong commitment and will work hard to preserve your relationship. There are some differences between you, but you're able to use this to your advantage. The American country partner's casual nature helps to loosen up the more formal traditionalist. The traditionalist brings an elegance and refinement that would otherwise be missing in the American country partner's life. Although the traditionalist tends to be insecure, she or he will feel reassured by the American country partner's honesty and loyalty. Both partners are sure to find happiness in this union.

| ORIENTAL | ORIENTAL | 6 |

Yours is a highly successful coupling. Both of you are very spiritual, each bringing a mystical element to your lives. You're constantly searching for and redefining the meaning of life. Other couples might achieve a greater degree of material success, but that's not important to either of you. You're much more concerned with exploring the world and experiencing all its beauty. A harmonious existence is something you both strive for. Fighting is a rare occurrence in a double-Orientalist relationship, since both partners treasure a peaceful and serene life-style. Most people would not be able to achieve such a compatible and fulfilling union, but the two of you have special qualities that make this kind of relationship possible.

ORIENTAL	ENGLISH COUNTRY	5

Y ou have a basic compatibility that results in a warm and relaxed relationship. Both of you favor a relatively low-key lifestyle that avoids stress and friction. The only potential problem is that the English country partner always wants to be surrounded by people, whereas the Orientalist needs some solitary time for his or her own thoughts. The Orientalist may balk at spending all of his or her free time with someone else no matter how much he or she loves the other person; the English country partner is apt to feel neglected and rebuffed by the Orientalist's insistence on private time and space. Fortunately, both of you are capable of calmly discussing this essential difference between you and can arrive at a compromise that will satisfy you both.

ORIENTAL	AMERICAN COUNTRY	5

Y ou're an interesting pair because you're very similar in some respects and quite different in others. Both of you want to live in a pure and simple manner. Other people may wish for fame and fortune, but not you two. You're happy just living productive, honest lives. But the simplicity that the Orientalist seeks is not anything like what the American country partner values. The Orientalist wants a life that focuses on spiritual knowledge and aesthetic accomplishments, whereas the American country partner wants to live in a more earthy manner, working with his or her hands to be as self-sufficient as possible. At times it may seem as if the American country partner's lack of sophistication is at odds with the Orientalist's cultural and intellectual development, but you manage to complement each other and lead a well-balanced life.

ENGLISH COUNTRY	ENGLISH COUNTRY	6

You're two of a kind! Both of you are well-adjusted people who are usually happy with their lives. You take great pleasure in the same things: good friends, stimulating music and literature, and interesting things to do in your spare time. You both want to enjoy life in a relaxed, tension-free manner. Because the two of you especially savor intimate conversation with the people you love, you've developed excellent communication skills and are able to share your innermost feelings better than most other couples. Each of you is very discriminating and wouldn't be happy with just any partner. It takes a very special person to fully satisfy someone who favors the English country style . . . and the ideal choice is another person who also appreciates the English country style.

ENGLISH COUNTRY	AMERICAN COUNTRY	4

The two of you are actually more similar than it might appear on the surface. What you both want is a happy, secure life with a stable partner. You both want a home filled with warmth and laughter. But there are some differences between you that can threaten your relationship. The English country partner continually strives to create a favorable impression among both strangers and friends, whereas the American country partner isn't the least bit concerned with matters relating to social status and reputation. Negative feelings may surface as the English country partner resents the American country counterpart for not being more helpful in social matters while the American country partner is annoyed by the English country partner's preoccupation with image and prestige. Your relationship can prosper only if you emphasize your similarities and accept the fact that you'll never share the same social needs.

AMERICAN COUNTRY	AMERICAN COUNTRY	6

Only a couple who both enjoy American country decor could have such a warm, loving relationship. You're best friends as well as lovers. Because honesty and integrity are mutual virtues, you know you can trust each other completely. You would never do anything to hurt the other person. Neither one of you is terribly interested in achieving success in the business world; instead, you prefer to devote your energies to making a happy home. You're not concerned about what other people think of you, so you can concentrate on just being yourselves. Making each other happy comes naturally to a dual-American country couple. Other couples may have reason to complain about their relationship, but you're blessed with a trouble-free, totally compatible union.

10

Food Preference

You are what you eat.

Like all familiar adages, there is more than a hint of truth in this simple sentence. The foods you choose to eat have a significant effect on the way your body and mind function. Your food choices also reveal something about your personality. It therefore follows that a preference for certain types of foods may have some bearing on a couple's compatibility. If you're into health food and your partner is a fast-food junkie, for example, you obviously may run into some difficulty at mealtime. But what about the nongastronomic aspects of your life together? Can a french-fry lover find happiness with a brown-rice eater?

Take the short quiz below to pinpoint your preferred eating styles, then find the section that addresses your combined types.

Quiz

You've both had a rough day at work. Nothing in your refrigerator is very appetizing and neither of you feels like shopping and cooking. Your partner tells you to choose a restaurant, saying

131

"Anything you pick is okay with me; choose whatever you think you'd enjoy."
Which one of these restaurants would each of you choose?

Restaurant A
Focuses on natural and vegetarian foods.

SAMPLE MENU: miso soup, mushroom-potato stew, stir-fried vegetables, brown rice, honey-wheat bread, frozen yogurt, herbal tea

Restaurant B
Offers typical fast-food items.

SAMPLE MENU: charbroiled burger, fried onion rings, fried chicken, coleslaw, chocolate milk shakes, doughnuts, ice cream

Restaurant C
Serves Continental cuisine, with emphasis on Italian and French specialties.

SAMPLE MENU: shrimp cocktail, truffle pâté, vichyssoise, caesar salad, veal piccata, sole Véronique, chocolate mousse

Restaurant D
Specializes in southern American home-style cooking.

SAMPLE MENU: chicken-noodle soup, meat loaf, turkey and dressing, mashed potatoes, tossed salad, black-eyed peas, blueberry cobbler

Person 1	Restaurant	Person 2
_____	A	_____
_____	B	_____
_____	C	_____
_____	D	_____

A A	6

You're a caring, supportive couple. You understand each other fully and are accepting of the other person's feelings. You both take the relationship seriously, but in a relaxed, easygoing way. Because you each know that you can trust your partner completely, you're able to fully share all aspects of your lives. You do need to make sure that you don't get into a rut with each other. Be open to new experiences and adventures that can add excitement to your relationship.

A B	5

The two of you are living proof that opposites attract and can be good for each other. The A's introspective tendencies are nicely counterbalanced by the B's outgoing nature. While the B inspires the A to become a little more dynamic and achievement-oriented, the A mellows the B and teaches him or her how to relax. If you both can be flexible and tolerant of each other's idiosyncrasies, there shouldn't be any major problems in your relationship.

A C	3

Although your personal styles are dramatically different, it *is* possible for you to enjoy a life together . . . as long as you're both willing to expend the effort needed to develop and maintain your relationship. Since there are so many intrinsic differences between you, you could easily drift apart if you don't devote sufficient time to work out the inevitable problems. You do share a tendency to be much more concerned with your individual selves than with your partner, but this is the only mutual characteristic. The A is more serious than the C and focuses on the totality of life rather than on the individual parts. The C lives in the present, while the A is future-oriented. Many of your values are different as well.

But if your love is strong enough, none of these problems will be insurmountable.

| A   D | 5 |

On the surface, you might appear to be a somewhat mismatched couple. The D is much more conservative and traditional than the A. The A is a dreamer while the D is pragmatic and realistic. But the two of you are similar in certain respects. You both want a relationship filled with warmth and comfort. You're both happiest in familiar situations with people you know well and care deeply about. Consequently, you each make a wonderfully loyal partner for the other.

| B   B | 2 |

The two of you are very much alike. This similarity is not necessarily beneficial to your relationship, however. The extremely competitive nature that you share can often lead to your working *against* each other rather than together as a team. Compromise does not come easily to either of you; you know exactly what you want and are determined to get it regardless of the consequences. You'd like to be more caring and supportive with each other, but your energies are scattered in too many other directions to really make the effort. If you want a more satisfying relationship than you currently have, you'll need to put some of your individual needs and interests on the back burner so that you can concentrate on your mutual concerns.

| B   C | 6 |

You complement each other in several ways. The B is active and interested in the world at large, but she or he tends to be conservative and cautious. The highly adventurous C can open up new horizons for the B partner. While the C exposes the B to a variety of different experiences, the B can help the C expand his or her emotional capacities and become more capable of sharing and caring. The C, who is very self-oriented, can use the B's strong sense of commitment to and involvement in the relationship as a foundation for expanding his or her focus beyond strictly personal concerns.

B D	**1**

You both are likely to experience extreme frustration in your relationship. The D's constant need for reassurance and support will probably not be met by a B partner. It's not that the B doesn't care; she or he simply isn't able to express it in the way the D would like. The active B has difficulty understanding the laid-back nature of the D. Resentment can result if the B feels that the D is holding him or her back in any way. B-D relationships can survive only if both partners make a significant effort to tolerate the other's personal style.

C C	**4**

When both partners are C's, it is a sure bet that they'll enjoy an exciting life together. The two of you are attracted to a lifestyle full of luxury and adventure. Other couples undoubtedly envy you for the glamour that is so much a part of you both. What they might not realize, however, is that appearances can be deceiving. You *don't* "have it all." What's missing in your lives is emotional intimacy. Your communication with each other tends to be superficial; in many ways you're nothing more than two acquaintances who happen to spend a lot of time together. To really become a couple, you'll need to develop better communication skills. Work to confide in each other about your innermost thoughts and feelings. Instead of talking about the multitude of extraneous details in your lives, focus on the issues that matter.

	C D		3

C-D relationships are a study in dramatic contrasts. If your relationship survives, it will be very successful; if it fails, it will fail in a big way. Seldom are problems between two people as black and white as yours are. The C is typically self-oriented whereas the D is more other-directed. This results in the D's perception of the C as being selfish and uncaring. The C in turn finds the D to be clinging and demanding. Another difference is the C's love of adventure versus the D's preference for familiarity. The D feels uncomfortable when the C pushes him or her into new experiences, while the C resents the D for limiting the excitement that is so important in a C's life. Mutual understanding and acceptance (important in *any* relationship) is critical for C and D partners.

	D D		6

A double-D couple can't miss! Only a D could understand another D's constant need for affection. The two of you are bound to be one of the most demonstrative and caring couples around. There is very little that can go astray in your relationship. But do watch out for outside interference. Other people may be jealous of what you have together and may try to sabotage it. Fortunately, you two are a close-knit unit that can't easily be broken.

11

Birth Experience

Freud considered the birth experience to be the origin of all anxieties that occur later in life. Labor and birth are typically very traumatic because they necessitate the first physical separation from the mother and the womb as well as force the first contact with the outside world. The specific birth experience is accompanied by an equally specific set of responses to the situation. This response tends to be repeated throughout an individual's life, predisposing him or her to think, feel, and behave a certain way.

Not all births are traumatic. Some (fortunate) babies just slip out with minimal physical and psychological discomfort. But according to two prominent experts in the field (Arthur Janov, author of *Imprints: The Life Long Effects of the Birth Experience*, New York: Putnam 1984; and Leslie Fehrer, author of *The Psychology of Birth*, New York; Continuum, 1981), many births are stressful enough to cause a psychic imprint that permanently impacts upon future personality traits. To analyze how your birth experiences affect the way in which you relate to each other, simply pinpoint the type of birth experiences you each had. Your mothers would be the ideal source of information about what actually occurred in your births. Then compare your answers to find your compatibility profile.

137

Forceps: Being pulled out of the womb with surgical instruments.

Delayed: Birth is delayed for some reason (e.g., stabilizing the mother's condition or the physician showing up late).

Prolonged: Labor may be light, but it persists for a long period of time. (The birth is allowed to occur naturally.)

Breech: Born with buttocks or legs first rather than headfirst.

Cesarean: Surgical removal through the mother's abdomen.

Premature: Born before normal nine-month gestation period.

Postmature: Born after normal nine-month gestation period.

Multiple Birth: In the case of twins, triplets, etc., see either delayed or prolonged labor (depending on the actual birth experience).

Normal: Textbook labor and birth, with none of the preceding complications.

Person 1	Birth experience	Person 1
_____	Forceps	_____
_____	Delayed	_____
_____	Prolonged	_____
_____	Breech	_____
_____	Cesarean	_____
_____	Premature	_____
_____	Postmature	_____
_____	Normal	_____

NOTE: You may have had more than one type of experience during your birth. For example, it is possible to be both postmature and breech. If this is the case, you'll need to check off both these birth experiences in your column. You'll then need to pair both these answers with those of your partner and read all the pertinent profiles. If your partner was both cesarean and postmature and you were postmature and breech, you'll need to read the cesarean-postmature, cesarean-breech, postmature-breech, and post-mature-postmature profiles. Each profile will reveal something about the different facets of your personalities and how they affect your relationship.

| FORCEPS   FORCEPS | 1 |

You're very much alike, but this can cause some problems in your dealings with each other. Because you'll tend to overintellectualize everything you experience together, you're in danger of never really feeling much of anything. Unless you make an extra effort to add adventure, laughter, and passion to your relationship, these joys will be sorely lacking in your lives. It's very possible that you'll both be so focused on achieving your long-term goals (e.g., your dream house or retirement) that you won't enjoy life—or each other—along the way. Still another concern is your mutual dependency. As individuals, you're each very unsure of your ability to stand on your own two feet. As a couple you may feed into each other's insecurities and wind up convincing yourselves that you can never be successful in life, especially on your own.

Fortunately, you both have the brain power to develop workable solutions to these problems. You can help each other feel more comfortable about expressing emotions, particularly the more positive ones. You can see to it that you engage in new experiences and enjoy the humorous aspects of life together. Also helpful is a focus on finding pleasure in the present rather than delaying it until the future. Above all, don't allow each other to dwell on anxieties. Provide encouragement and support so that your partner can begin to achieve some of his or her individual potential.

| FORCEPS   DELAYED | 1 |

It's imperative for you both to be aware of the problem dynamics that are likely to occur in your relationship. The forceps partner's tendency to intellectualize can frustrate the highly emotional delayed-birth partner. This isn't entirely the forceps partner's fault. The delayed individual is very susceptible to emotional upsets and fears, and it's difficult for any partner ever to make him or her feel really secure. Together the two of you are likely to convince yourselves that other people can have success in the world but not you. This will result in your letting others take the lead instead of taking control of your own lives.

But if both of you are willing to make some changes, you can improve your individual life situations as well as your relationship. Encourage each other to take risks. Playing it safe will result in things continuing as they are and chances are that neither of you really wants this. To find fulfillment together, allow the forceps partner to brainstorm additional techniques for getting what you both want out of life and being in charge of your own destinies. The forceps must also be careful never to give any reason for the delayed partner to feel that she or he has been abandoned by a disinterested lover. Both of you (but especially the forceps) need to be attentive to and supportive of each other.

FORCEPS   PROLONGED   1

Each of you wants entirely different things out of life. The forceps partner is totally goal-oriented. She or he doesn't care how she or he gets there; all that's important is the getting there. The prolonged partner, on the other hand, values the *process* and isn't the least bit concerned about setting or reaching any goals. Obviously, with two such divergent orientations your approaches to everything in your lives are quite dissimilar.

If the one thing you do agree on is that you want a long-term relationship, you'll need to become expert at the art of compromising and negotiating. You won't be able to develop mutually satisfactory solutions all the time, but you can make a special effort to take both your needs into account in whatever you do together. If you can't do this simultaneously, then take turns satisfying each other's needs. Lovemaking can serve as an excellent illustration of this strategy. The forceps partner usually wants to rush into and quickly complete the act, while the prolonged partner enjoys every moment and prefers it to last as long as possible. The solution is for the two of you to alternate "quickies" with long, sensual lovemaking sessions. Using this approach in all areas of your lives can help you live and love happily together.

FORCEPS	BREECH		2

You're bound to have several problems in this relationship. The forceps personality is highly intellectual, whereas the breech partner undervalues cognition. Brains are important to the forceps partner; the breech is more concerned with bodily skills (as manifested in athletics or sexuality). Both of you tend to be unemotional. This shared trait enables you to avoid quarreling like other couples over small things, but it also results in a somewhat cold and distant relationship.

Further difficulties may occur as a consequence of the breech's aggression. The breech wants to be in control, but when allowed to take charge, she or he becomes very anxious and may behave in an irrational and even hostile manner. The forceps partner lacks self-confidence and doesn't have the fortitude to defend against the breech's wrath. For the most part your lives should be fairly calm, except when the breech is unhappy about something. If the breech can learn to cope with his or her negative feelings in a more constructive way, you'll both fare better in your dealings with each other.

FORCEPS	CESAREAN		2

Dependency is one of the most significant characteristics of your relationship. Both of you are afraid to be your own persons. You'd each prefer to cling to someone else than develop competence as an individual. While it does provide you with a sense of comfort to have a partner who feels the same way you do, it doesn't encourage either of you to take the first steps toward independence.

Aside from your mutual dependency, there isn't very much you share in common. The cesarean personality desires to live as simple and uncomplicated a life as possible. She or he shies away from learning new ways of doing things, even if they promise to make life better. This is in sharp contrast to the intellectual forceps partner, who takes great pleasure in acquiring new knowledge. At times the forceps partner will find his or her cesarean counterpart to be mentally unstimulating and may yearn for a partner who can engage in more challenging conversations. The forceps individual is also apt to feel that the cesarean's irresponsibility prevents him or her from being a dependable companion. Thus, a cesarean-forceps union can be less than ideal for both partners but is particularly unfulfilling for the forceps individual unless you both work to address these pitfalls.

FORCEPS	PREMATURE	4

The premature-birth individual can help the forceps personality develop more self-confidence. Because the premature partner is determined not to be held back by any external barriers, she or he is an excellent role model for the easily discouraged forceps individual who usually doesn't believe that control of his or her own fate is possible. The association with a premature personality can be just what the forceps partner needs to begin to participate in life, taking some risks to reap some rewards.

But there are negative aspects to your relationship as well. Your social life as a couple will be dismal because neither of you has acquired the skills to form close friendships. You both have limited sensual natures and consequently won't experience the passionate lovemaking known to other couples. These may not be significant problems, however, since your social or sexual lives are not a priority for either of you.

FORCEPS	POSTMATURE	4

The forceps personality will benefit from the postma-ture-birth individual's strength and independence since these are qualities the forceps lacks. The postmature's ability to set his or her own agenda without worrying about what anyone will think can be an inspiration to the forceps individual. When paired with a post-mature partner, the forceps may finally attempt to become his or her own person, even when the chances for success appear limited.

The postmature's realism should also prove to be extremely helpful for the forceps individual, who has a tendency to fantasize rather than objectively analyze a situation.

The only potential trouble area is that the postmature personality's aversion to confinement can be so strong that she or he may resist making an emotional commitment. While the postmature partner may feel trapped by a long-term monogamous relationship, this is exactly what the forceps individual wants. The forceps partner's insecurity makes him or her need a partner to count on. Since your relationship does have many positive aspects, see if you can work out a compromise between the forceps's need for total commitment and the postmature's desire for freedom.

FORCEPS	NORMAL		2

The normal-birth personality doesn't have any inner turmoils of his or her own, but may have difficulty dealing with those of the forceps-birth partner. At first the forceps's intellectualizing may be endearing, but the normal-birth individual may eventually resent the overemphasis on thinking with the head rather than feeling with the heart. The normal-birth partner may also not appreciate the forceps-birth partner's lack of competence and confidence, deficiencies that cause the forceps to be dependent on the more self-assured normal-birth individual. You'll have to be sensitive to each other's needs to make this relationship work.

DELAYED	DELAYED		3

Two delayed-birth individuals undoubtedly have an extremely close relationship. This closeness tends to border on the pathological, however, The two of you cling to each other, not out of love so much as for safety. Your insecurity grows to unmanageable proportions if you don't have someone who can provide you with constant support and protection. You share the same fears of the world; you both are afraid of what life may bring. Consequently, you avoid as much interaction with other people and with external events as possible, concentrating instead on yourselves.

You form a tight little unit that effectively manages to keep outsiders far away. This is exactly what you both desire, but neither of you realizes that it limits your growth as individuals. You'll tend to remain stagnant throughout your entire lives. If one of you occasionally gets an urge to be more independent and take a few more risks, the other will experience a great deal of anxiety. This will lead to the first partner feeling guilty about even thinking about trying to become his or her own person. This relationship will be a happy one, but remember you'll both benefit by putting more of an emphasis on growth.

DELAYED PROLONGED	4

Your relationship should generally proceed more smoothly than many other pairings because you share similar needs and personality styles. Neither of you is interested in setting the world on fire with your achievements; you'd much rather enjoy your lives in a leisurely way. You both find comfort in familiarity, often going to great lengths to avoid anything you don't know. Together you can establish a comfortable life-style and a cozy home environment.

But you may occasionally experience some slight static in your relationship. When the delayed-birth partner becomes too clinging and possessive, the prolonged-birth partner may resent that dependency if it interferes with what's become established as your orderly lives. The prolonged personality wants to conduct everything (even his or her emotional affairs) in a carefully regimented manner. If the delayed partner makes too many demands and upsets the routine, the prolonged partner may become extremely unhappy. Consequently, it behooves the delayed-birth partner to work on developing a little more independence.

DELAYED   BREECH   3

There are many concerns that you have in common. You're both insecure when it comes to the important people in your lives. You very much want to be able to count on your significant others, but you never feel completely comfortable in doing so. As much as you want to have a special closeness, you find it difficult to completely trust someone else. You also share ambiguous feelings about being independent. You'd like to be in charge of your own individual destinies, but because you're not convinced that you can do so on your own, you become dependent on whomever you can. What is different about the two of you is how you each deal with not getting what you need or want. The delayed-birth partner becomes passive and withdrawn, whereas the breech-birth individual may overreact and even show aggression.

It's up to the two of you to decide the outcome of your relationship. You can allow your anxieties to escalate, feeding off each other until you're both miserable. Or you could resolve to help each other learn to deal with your concerns and worries. With sufficient determination and strength, you can develop more optimal coping mechanisms and healthier patterns of thinking and relating.

DELAYED   CESAREAN   3

Your relationship has both positive and negative aspects. On the down side, you have a mutual problem with dependency. You both question your competence in most areas of your lives and feel that you need to rely on others for support. Neither one of you is proficient at setting your own goals and accomplishing them. As a couple, you're likely to be continually struggling to achieve what other pairings seem to get almost effortlessly.

But your situation has its good side. You can be quite helpful to each other. Whereas the delayed-birth partner is apt to be frozen in a state of perpetual inertia, the cesarean-birth personality doesn't hesitate to take action. Thus the cesarean can inspire the delayed partner to ignore any perceived restrictions or constraints and go for whatever she or he wants. Because the delayed-birth partner treasures emotional closeness, he or she can bring a level of intimacy that would otherwise be missing in the cesarean-birth partner's life. Trying to capitalize on your strong points while minimizing your weaker ones (important for any couple) is crucial for you two.

DELAYED   PREMATURE   **3**

The premature-birth individual is fortunate in one specific regard to have a delayed-birth partner. The lack of social skills associated with the premature personality can be counterbalanced by the delayed-partner's emphasis on warm interpersonal ties. With the delayed-birth partner regularly reaching out to him or her, the premature-birth partner can't help but respond in a loving manner. Emotional sharing may not come readily to the premature personality, but in time he or she may be an appropriate responsive partner.

What you need to watch out for is that the premature personality doesn't drag both of you down with his or her irresponsibility. The premature-birth partner typically doesn't make wise or mature decisions. This obviously can get him or her as well as any close association into trouble. The delayed-birth partner is a particularly likely candidate for such occurrences, since she or he tends to take a passive role in a relationship. A delayed will overlook a partner's transgressions just to keep the peace. As far as the delayed-birth partner is concerned, it is preferable to accept the premature's shortcomings than to become vocal about them and possibly risk losing the partner. If the two of you intend to maintain a long-term relationship, the delayed-birth partner *must* learn to develop enough gumption to refuse to go along with the premature's foolhardy schemes.

DELAYED	POSTMATURE	5

Your pairing can be ideal for both of you. The postmature-birth partner has a chance to use his or her leadership ability with the submissive delayed-birth individual (who is only too happy to let someone else rule his or her life). Rather than simply wishing for things to happen, the delayed-birth individual can be helped by the postmature partner to find the initiative to make things happen. The postmature personality can enable the delayed to stop getting discouraged by real or perceived constraints and instead do something about them.

But your relationship can fizzle if the delayed-birth partner becomes overly clinging and demanding. The postmature personality doesn't want a partner who is going to place any restrictions on him or her. Learning to become less needy would be extremely helpful for the delayed-birth personality; this would be a small price for the delayed-birth individual to pay in comparison to the benefits of having such a dynamic partner.

DELAYED	NORMAL	2

The delayed-birth partner's need for closeness is so pronounced that it can make the normal-birth partner withdraw from all that emotional intensity. While the normal-birth partner doesn't have any problems with intimacy, he or she is too much of his or her own person to tolerate the delayed-birth individual, who can function more as a clinging vine than as an equal partner. The delayed-birth personality's fear of abandonment leads him or her to want to be with the normal-birth partner on a nonstop basis, constantly sharing the deepest fears and desires of both individuals. This is likely to become too much for the normal-birth partner, and the delayed-birth is well advised to try to restrain his or her dependent impulses so that the relationship will be happier in the long term.

PROLONGED	PROLONGED	6

The two of you are virtually identical in every way and should fit well together. You can maintain a leisurely life with each other where you don't attempt to prove anything or to accomplish fantastic feats. You're happy just *being*, enjoying each day as it happens without any undue pressures. This is the way you both choose to live, and it's definitely right for you two.

But there are some drawbacks to being a pair of prolonged-birth individuals. As individuals and as a couple, you'll procrastinate every chance you get. Whenever possible, you'll put off making decisions and taking any action. Needless to say, you won't wind up achieving what some other couples do. And while it's true that you both favor order and ritual as the prime ingredients in your daily lives, you'll be missing out on a great deal by never opening yourselves to things that are new or unexpected. Try to help each other get to the point where you can be comfortable without planning every moment of your lives to run in an orderly, predictable fashion. If you can do this, you'll be one of the happiest, best-adjusted couples around.

PROLONGED	BREECH	4

You two won't experience any overwhelming problems, but your relationship might also lack some sparks. In general, things will be pretty peaceful. Neither of you wants a real challenge. You both prefer a life that's relatively undemanding. You don't want to have to continually think about your daily activities or to be pressed to solve a lot of problems. Both of you choose to conserve your physical and intellectual energies as much as you can.

But there is some potential for discord in your relationship. Much of this is due to the breech-birth's partner's tendency to blow things out of proportion. If the breech-birth individual is displeased by something the prolonged-birth partner has done, she or he is likely to overreact and become extremely angry. Naturally, this can be disconcerting to the prolonged-birth individual (especially since the breech-birth partner is typically passive, these bouts of aggression come as a great shock). If the breech-birth partner can learn to more appropriately express his or her anger, you'd both be better off.

| PROLONGED   CESAREAN | 5 |

You share the same desire for a hassle-free, low-stress life-style. To a large extent, you should be able to achieve this kind of life together. The order and ritual that are so important to the prolonged-birth partner are usually agreeable to the cesarean-birth personality because it guarantees an uncomplicated existence with little necessity to learn new things. A challenge is not something that either of you seeks. You want to make things as easy as possible for yourselves, so you avoid the demands, trappings, and game-playing that other couples are involved with.

The only real difference between you two is that the cesarean-birth personality may occasionally want to do something on the spur of the moment simply because it sounds appealing at the time. Such spontaneity is very threatening to the prolonged-birth partner since it prevents him or her from planning and procrastinating (the two most frequent activities of a prolonged-birth personality). On rare occasions, the cesarean-birth partner may exhibit a propensity for drama at times, and this is another trait that can be unnerving to the prolonged-birth individual. Although this dramatic urge doesn't surface too often in the cesarean partner, the prolonged partner will be stunned and unhappy by any sudden displays of unconventional or unrestrained behavior. If the two of you can learn to fully express your feelings and attempt to see them from the other's point of view, you'll be able to deal with your problems as they (infrequently) occur.

| PROLONGED   PREMATURE | 4 |

All too often, you'll find yourselves at cross-purposes. The prolonged-birth personality is uncomfortable without a lot of structure in his or her life, whereas the premature-birth individual resents any restrictions or constraints placed on him or her. The premature-birth personality's desire to be free of external controls is the polar opposite of the prolonged-birth partner's need for outside support and order. Obviously this presents problems since the premature rebels against being tied down, while the prolonged desperately clings to whatever is familiar.

But this relationship does have the potential to work, provided you each allow the other to seek what she or he needs. The premature-birth personality must be given the freedom to act on his or her whims, even when the prolonged-birth partner considers such action to be unwarranted or even foolhardy. The prolonged-birth partner has to be given the opportunity to live with clearly defined boundaries and well-developed support systems. While the premature personality doesn't need close ties with friends and family, she or he must accept that the prolonged partner does have these needs and allow them to be fulfilled. If the premature personality feels too confined, the prolonged has to understand the premature's need to escape, whether by a night out alone or separate vacations. A high degree of empathy and cooperation from both of you is essential for a prolonged—premature pairing to fulfill its potential.

PROLONGED	POSTMATURE	5

For the most part, you'll be able to live together in harmony. You're both fun-loving people who are determined to get all you can out of your lives. Neither of you is overly concerned about the future; you prefer to let the future take care of itself and instead devote your efforts to maximum enjoyment of the present. As a result of these philosophies, your relationship will be a happy one in which you dedicate yourselves to making a satisfying life together.

However, there is one potential trouble spot for you. The prolonged partner needs a great deal of structure in his or her life. Spontaneity scares him or her because it can lead to unpredictable outcomes. The prolonged would much rather have an orderly life in which everything is carefully planned out. But this doesn't work well for the postmature personality. Postmature tends to feel trapped and even panicky when there are these demands for order.

The postmature-birth partner prefers to feel enough autonomy to guide his or her own life without having all the events and people rigidly proscribed without any room for deviation. Compromise is the only solution to this essential difference between you. You each have to be willing to give in and give up a little for the sake of your partnership.

PROLONGED NORMAL	5

The two of you can relate fairly well to each other. The normal-birth partner can serve as an excellent role model for the prolonged-birth individual, showing him or her how to get things done instead of always procrastinating. Thanks to the normal-birth partner, you'll be able to set goals for yourselves (instead of the prolonged-birth partner's haphazard involvement with different activities and events). Occasionally, the normal-birth partner may wish for more spontaneity from the prolonged-birth partner, but can usually maintain a positive attitude about the prolonged partner's need for order and ritual. The normal-birth partner may even find him- or herself enjoying the stability that the prolonged-birth personality adds to his or her life.

BREECH BREECH	2

Yours is a difficult pairing. Because you both have your share of emotional conflicts and problems that you continually need to work through, there will tend to be a lot of friction and static in your relationship. Both of you feel the need to try to control others. This obviously is a trait that will cause resentment in the other person and chances are she or he will rebel against such attempts at power. It's quite possible for the two of you to become very aggressive in your struggle to assume authority.

You're both more action-oriented than intellectually or emotionally inclined. Consequently, your communication with each other will be limited. Instead of expressing your emotions, you'll act (sometimes impulsively) on them and leave your respective partners guessing as to why you're behaving that way. When you eventually are forced to acknowledge and attempt to deal with your feelings, you'll find that there are a lot of unresolved issues as well as ambiguity that you each need to work out. Your relationship is not impossible, but it does require commitment and dedication to make a go of it.

BREECH	CESAREAN	3

Several issues will present challenges for your relationship. The first is that of dependence versus self-reliance. The breech-birth partner is a very capable individual who readily takes charge and makes things happen on his or her own. The cesarean-birth personality, on the other hand, is totally dependent on others for everything in life. This has the potential to become a burden on the breech-birth partner, who may try to encourage the cesarean-birth partner to take more control of his or her own life, but the cesarean is likely to make only feeble attempts at doing so. If the cesarean-birth personality meets with any difficulties or complications, she or he will immediately give up. The cesarean's lack of perseverance is another issue that demands attention in your relationship because the breech-birth personality will find it difficult to respect a partner with so little determination.

But there can be an optimistic prognosis for your relationship. The breech-birth partner does like to control and manipulate others, something that can be readily done with a cesarean partner. If the cesarean-birth personality continues to look to the breech-birth partner for decision-making and guidance, the breech-birth individual will tend to be flattered and to relish the power. Provided the breech-birther doesn't take unfair advantage of the cesarean-birth counterpart, the two of you may manage to get both your needs met in this relationship.

BREECH	PREMATURE	5

The two of you are quite compatible. You both prefer to neglect your individual development and instead get wrapped up in the trivia of your everyday lives. Experimenting with different lifestyles or learning new things is not appealing to either of you. You'd much rather live your lives as they are than to develop alternative approaches or face challenges. You also share a preference for a limited social life. Neither of you has developed good skills in relating to other people, so you're more comfortable by yourselves.

The premature-birth personality will undoubtedly be the more passive partner in the relationship because she or he doesn't want to assume any independence or responsibility. She or he is more than happy letting the breech-birth partner take command. This in turn pleases the breech-birth partner, who feels a strong need for power. While other people might not be happy in your kind of relationship, it suits both of you just fine.

BREECH	POSTMATURE	1

Some conflicts will be inevitable in your relationship. You both want to be in charge at all times. When there are occasions where only one of you can be in a leadership role, neither of you will gracefully transfer to a subordinate one. Instead, you're likely to fight furiously to be the one with the power. For a while you both may enjoy this struggle. At first it may seem like an invigorating challenge that demands you be on your toes and strive to be at your best. But you may eventually discover that these power struggles can become energy-draining and stressful.

Therefore, you must both learn to channel your competitive natures into more constructive outlets. Find other people to compete against; become involved in activities that allow you to strive to be the victor. Learn to be assertive with each other rather than aggressive. Remember that winning can be gratifying, but it's a hollow victory if the person you love loses. A good relationship emphasizes win-win situations, so develop your skill at negotiating.

If you can tone down your cutthroat instincts, you can enjoy a dynamic relationship.

BREECH NORMAL	1

The breech-birther can be a difficult partner for anyone. She or he has many unresolved conflicts that need to be worked out. These concerns may have prevented the breech-birth individual from reaching his or her intellectual and emotional potential. Still another problem in any relationship involving a breech-birther is his or her ambiguity. At times the breech-birth individual will give the impression of wanting a lot of support and assistance from a partner; however, if the partner attempts to provide this help, the breech-birther is apt to rebuff these overtures and stubbornly insist on going it alone.

Fortunately, the normal-birth individual's excellent mental health puts him or her in an ideal position to help a breech-birth partner. The normal-birther will be able to cope with the breech-birther's insecurities and will consider it well worth the effort since the breech-birth partner's spontaneity and nonconformity makes him or her a challenging lover and companion. For the breech-birther's part, she or he must learn to accept the normal-birther's guidance and support. Working hard together will enable you to establish a satisfactory relationship in addition to developing the breech-birther's potential.

CESAREAN CESAREAN	4

It is a sure bet that two cesarean-birth personalities will have a dynamic relationship that never really settles down. You both are spontaneous, creative people who enjoy inventing things as you go. You enjoy the element of surprise and the freedom to act out your feelings at any given moment.

But as appealing as that aspect of your shared natures is, there are other qualities that you both have that are very likely to cause problems in your relationship. You both have difficulty handling responsibility. When things become too complicated, neither one of you wants to deal with them. If you don't succeed at something you attempt, the cesarean will blame it on someone else (never yourself). It is possible that you won't achieve any long-term success as a couple because of this mutual tendency to shy away from the necessities and realities of life. You won't do much in terms of helping each other mature, but you'll be comfortable together.

CESAREAN PREMATURE	4

Although you're not completely alike, there are many similarities. Neither of you is interested in assuming much responsibility; you prefer to enjoy life with as few complications as possible. You both neglect your intellectual capabilities, tending to avoid thinking about important issues in favor of simply experiencing your life as it unfolds. While you may get along well with each other for the most part, your social skills are not highly developed and you'll tend to be overly dependent on each other as a substitution for a wider circle of friends.

There is one important difference between you, and it is one that benefits the cesarean. The premature-birth partner usually denies or overlooks any external restrictions. If she or he wants to do something, it'll be done even if other people advise against it or there seems to be some sort of insurmountable barrier. This is in contrast to the cesarean's characteristic of giving up immediately when things appear difficult. Were it not for the premature-birth personality's fearlessness in going after what she or he needs or wants, the two of you would tend to be quite passive and would never achieve anything in life. Fortunately, this premature-birth characteristic enables you to have a relatively successful life together.

CESAREAN	POSTMATURE	5

Yours will be a relationship where one partner is clearly dominant (the postmature-birth individual) and the other assumes a subordinate role (the cesarean-birth personality). The postmature-birth partner provides strength and leadership to the dependent, somewhat helpless cesarean-birth partner. Rather than resenting this guidance, the cesarean-birth individual will be grateful for it and treat the postmature-birth partner with reverence.

This is not to imply that you'll have a completely one-sided relationship in which one partner gives and the other takes. To the contrary, the cesarean-birth personality has something special to add to the postmature-birth partner's life. The postmature-birth individual is very firmly grounded in reality and lacks the imaginative nature of the cesarean-birth partner. The relationship with the cesarean-birth individual can encourage the postmature-birth partner to become a little more adventurous and experiment with new means of self-expression. Thus, both of you are very likely to be pleased with your relationship.

CESAREAN	NORMAL	4

The cesarean-birth personality does not lend itself to being the ideal mate for a normal-birther, but there's still a good chance that your relationship can work out. Although the cesarean-birth partner may hesitate to fully develop his or her learning capacities, the normal-birth individual can function as an excellent teacher and show how to make the most of the cesarean's innate capabilities. And while the cesarean-birther tends toward dependency and a low tolerance for frustration, the normal-birther can encourage him or her to tough it out and to become more self-reliant. What the cesarean-birth partner doesn't need encouragment for is the dramatic; she or he knows how to live with a unique spontaneous flair. This gift for adding some spice to your relationship is something that can be wholeheartedly enjoyed by the normal-birth partner.

PREMATURE	PREMATURE	1

You're as similar as any two people can be . . . so you need to be careful not to duplicate your weaknesses. You'll both be very resistant to change, clinging to the status quo and each other for dear life. You share the same problem with maintaining friendships; neither of you knows how to reach out to someone else in a way that isn't overly demanding or suffocating. There is also a mutual lack of interest in developing your cognitive abilities to their fullest potential.

If you're going to stay together, resolve right now to get yourselves out of the rut you seem to be getting deeper and deeper into. Encourage each other to take some new risks and responsibilities. Learn to be close without crowding each other. A good way to pursue this goal is to study other successful couples to discover how they maintain their own individuality while still forming a successful union. Giving each other sufficient freedom is essential. And even if you have to force yourselves, begin to develop your intellects so that you can become challenging companions for each other.

PREMATURE	POSTMATURE	2

The postmature-birth individual is exactly the sort of partner that the premature-birth individual desperately needs. The postmature-birth personality possesses the maturity that the premature birth partner lacks. Knowing exactly who he or she is and where he or she is headed in life, the postmature-birth partner is well able to provide self-direction in addition to assisting a partner in doing the same. The postmature-birth partner's reality orientation and natural leadership skills make him or her a logical teacher for the premature-birth partner, who is much more apt to flounder around aimlessly without real direction.

But the benefits of your association are not reciprocal. The premature-birth individual doesn't have much to offer the postmature-birth individual. At most, the premature-birther provides a willing subject for the postmature-birth partner to dominate and thus satisfy this need for power. But it is entirely too likely that the premature-birth personality will become unbearably dependent on the postmature-birther, which can lead to the postmature's wanting to escape from the relationship. Your pairing can succeed only if the premature-birth partner exercises some restraint and is careful not to overburden the postmature-birther with never-ending needs.

PREMATURE	NORMAL	3

Your relationship has a fair chance of survival, although the normal-birther is apt to experience frequent exasperation with the premature-birth partner. The main problem will be the premature's immaturity. Like Peter Pan, the premature fears growing up and will rebel against behaving like an adult. Depending on the normal-birth partner's perspective, this can either be a charming trait that keeps you both young or it could become a headache that places the burden of your responsibilities upon the normal-birther. The normal-birth partner's natural inclination is to be protective of the premature-birther; this is something that makes the premature very comfortable, but it is something that should be discouraged for both your sakes. Instead, work hard together to function as *equals* in the relationship.

POSTMATURE	POSTMATURE	3

There's a lot to be said for your relationship—both good and bad. On the positive side, you share the same independent, strong-willed natures. Neither of you will ever have to worry about a helplessly dependent partner. Instead, you'll both be free to do your own things without being dragged down by someone who lacks direction in his or her life. You two know exactly who you are. You accept your innate personality traits and don't need to subject yourselves or a partner to the turmoil of searching for the "real you."

But there's an equal potential for a troubled relationship when two postmature-birth personalities are involved. You can both be unhealthily aggressive with each other and even forget that you're in love while you each concentrate your individual efforts on gaining the upper hand. As much as you may like having a strong partner, neither of you can easily relinquish the leadership role, even on a temporary basis. You also share a fear of confinement, and this sometimes translates to a fear of commitment. You each may feel trapped when you become intimate with someone else. Instead of calmly discussing your apprehensions, you're likely to deal with the situation by overreacting and completely withdrawing from each other. For a double-postmature relationship to succeed, you need to closely examine the dynamics of your relationship and be dedicated enough to expend sufficient energy to solve your mutual problems.

POSTMATURE   NORMAL   **5**

Your relationship comes with a very strong promise of success. You're both bright, strong individuals. You can each do well on your own, but when you combine forces you're guaranteed a productive, happy life. Only minor troubles such as occasional power struggles in which you both compete to be the dominant partner should occur in your relationship. There may also be some inappropriate (but, fortunately, infrequent) emotional responses (such as overreacting or withdrawing) from the postmature-birther when you encounter rough spots. But the two of you can weather out any insignificant turbulence and maintain your loving union.

NORMAL   NORMAL   **6**

Congratulations! As far as your birth experience goes, neither of you has suffered any major trauma and consequently has not brought any emotional baggage into the relationship. There should be nothing that interferes with your ability to have a happy life together.

Body Types

Psychologist William Sheldon believed that a person's body structure spoke of his or her personality. By analyzing the human physique, Sheldon found three basic components of body structure: endomorph (component of roundness), mesomorph (component of muscularity), and ectomorph (component of length). He then postulated that these structures are each linked with certain unique traits of temperament.

According to Sheldon, all three components are present in every physique and every psyche. No one can be considered a pure endomorph, for example; there would also be some ectomorphic and mesomorphic qualities in terms of body build and personality. But there is a dominant component in each of us as well as a secondary component.

Each of you needs to take the following quiz to pinpoint your dominant body type. (Be honest in answering these questions! Don't choose an answer that describes the way you'd like to be; choose the one that is most accurate. Some couples find their partner can answer these questions best for them.)

1. My general body contours are:
   A. soft and round
   B. hard and muscular
   C. long and thin

2. My head is:
   A. large, round, and full-faced
   B. large and square
   C. small or elongated and narrow
3. My neck is:
   A. short
   B. wide and thick
   C. long and slender
4. My torso is:
   A. wider toward the bottom, with a prominent belly
   B. well-developed and muscular, tapering down to a flat stomach
   C. narrow and flat, short in comparison to arms and legs
5. My arms are:
   A. full, soft, and rounded
   B. muscular
   C. long and slender
6. My hands have:
   A. small wrists and short fingers
   B. heavy wrists and thick, large-knuckled fingers
   C. slender wrists, with long, narrow fingers
7. My legs are:
   A. fleshy and curvy
   B. muscular
   C. thin, with the lower legs longer than the thighs
8. My hair is:
   A. fine-textured and fairly sparse
   B. coarse
   C. fine-textured but thick in quantity
9. My skin is:
   A. pale, ruddy, or rosy, soft, smooth
   B. thick, coarse, easily tanned
   C. thin, prone to extreme dryness, oiliness, or sensitivity

Record the number of times you each chose each letter.

Person 1	_____	_____	_____
	A	B	C
Person 2	_____	_____	_____
	A	B	C

Most of your answers will probably fall under one letter, denoting your dominant body type. If your answers are equally divided among all three letters, use your answer for #1 since this is the most revealing of all your answers. Combine your dominant letters to find your compatibility profile. You may also want to combine your secondary components as well. For example, if one of you had 6 A's and 3 B's and the other had 4 A's and 5 B's, your primary combination is A-B. However, person 1 has a secondary B component and person 2 has a secondary A component, so you may also want to look at the combinations of B-C and A-A, as well as B-A for some additional insights into how you relate in terms of your less dominant characteristics.

Person 1	Type	Person 2
_____	A	_____
_____	B	_____
_____	C	_____

A A		4

Two A's will always have a good time together. Both of you are born hedonists, seeking out all of life's pleasures. As far as you're concerned, there's no need to suffer or even work hard when there's so much fun to be had. You both thoroughly enjoy whatever makes you feel good, so you joyously partake in eating and sexual activity without any reservations or guilt. Comfort is another big priority with both of you. You seek to make your lives as easy and painless as possible.

Emotionally, you're both very stable. Although you express your emotions easily (crying or laughing without inhibition), you're generally quite calm. It takes a lot to get you upset, but you don't try to hide it when it happens. Instead, you make sure you discuss it with each other and work out a solution to get things back on the right track so life can feel good again.

Because you care so deeply about people in general, it's very easy for you to bond with one special person in particular. A's make extremely loyal and loving partners. In a dual-A pairing, there is little likelihood that either of you would ever stray. When you commit to someone, you want it to be long-term. Change isn't something you enjoy, so the last thing you'd want is a different partner. Once you become intimate with someone, you have no desire to ever be with anyone else. It's much more comfortable to stick with the tried and true, even if that person isn't perfect. Being practical-minded, with your feet firmly planted on the ground, you know there's no such thing as an ideal partner . . . only one who understands you and accepts you just as you are.

You share a common desire to surround yourselves with other people. You greatly enjoy parties and other social occasions. Large crowds don't bother you at all; in fact, you thrive on the opportunity to be with so many. Both of you will go to great lengths to avoid being alone. You feel that all activities should be shared with someone else. You hate the thought of eating and drinking by yourselves, so you'll be sure to provide constant companionship for each other as well as to encircle yourselves with as many friends as possible.

But there is a down side to your temperament. You can both be extremely possessive, demanding that you spend every waking moment together. And although there's a lot of love in an A-A relationship, there isn't much opportunity for personal growth. You're both very conservative, clinging to the traditional and familiar. Change makes you uncomfortable; you'll stick with what you know well, whether it's people, ideas, or behavior. Further compounding the problem is your mutual tendency to conform. You'll go along with the group and won't ever take a stand on your own. So as long as you're together and reinforcing the traits you have in common, it's unlikely that you'll ever develop your individual selves. But there's no question that you will have a strong, caring, all-consuming relationship.

| A   B | 3 |

Although you're quite different from each other, it's still possible that your relationship can work. The A will need to work on being a little less dependent so that the B can have some breathing space. If the A expects the B to always be at his or her side, the A will be sorely disappointed. Unlike the A, the B doesn't need to be with people all the time. The A tends to find solitude scary, but this doesn't have to be a problem. Because the A has so many other friends, she or he can spend time with them while the B does his or her own thing.

Another reason that the B can't be with the A all the time is that you don't like to do the same things in your spare time. The A prefers to relax while the B enjoys physical challenges. The thought of working out at the gym or climbing a mountain is horrifying to the A but immensely appealing to the B. There's no way that the B can be happy just sitting at home all the time; she or he needs to be actively involved in things that involve some risk and adventure. The B will become resentful if the A insists that the B forgo such activities, so the A will need to accept the B's needs and find other ways to fulfill his or her own needs.

The A can easily express his or her feelings, but this is not the case with the B. The B uses action rather than words to deal with his or her emotions. Therefore, the B will go out of his or her way to express love for the A by giving gifts or doing nice things, but will seldom say "I love you." The A can verbalize whatever is on his or her mind but will have to be careful not to overwhelm the B with too many intense declarations and discussions.

It may sound like the A is the one who has to make all the compromises and sacrifices in your relationship. This is correct. The B tends to be more stubborn and assertive, refusing to change his or her ways. Fortunately, the A's generous nature enables him or her to yield to the wants of the B for the sake of staying together. Since the A is naturally more passive, she or he doesn't mind letting the B dominate the relationship. But lest it sound as if the B is the only one who benefits from your pairing, keep in mind that the A receives a great deal from the B in return. Because the B is so much more energetic and ambitious than the A, the B will experience more success in the work world. Consequently, the B makes an excellent provider and allows the A to live in more luxury and with more ease (two things that are very important to the A) than an A would be able to manage without a B partner. The B can also help the A break out of what can become a boringly predictable existence. The A may be uncomfortable at first if the B exposes him or her to different types of people and new adventures, but the A will gradually find that his or her life has been enriched.

You're mirror opposites of each other. The C tends to be fearful and even pessimistic about life, while the A looks forward to every day with relentless optimism. The A greatly enjoys conversation, but the C prefers to harbor his or her own thoughts. Still another difference is that the C is high-strung while the A is calm by nature.

The list of differences continues. The C likes everything in his or her own life to go quickly. He or she doesn't want to waste time taking longer than needed to eat, sleep, walk, talk, or even make love. This is in sharp contrast to the languorous A, who likes to savor every activity and make it last as long as possible.

Your social natures are entirely different as well. The C likes to spend a great deal of time alone with his or her own thoughts and despises large parties and other situations where it's necessary to be around a lot of other people. But the A is very gregarious and is unhappy being alone. She or he looks forward to social occasions.

You'll never be exactly on the same wavelength . . . and that can be good. You both tend toward extremes in temperament and this isn't always healthy. As a couple you can work toward developing more of a balance. Learn to compromise and merge some of your personality traits together. For example, the A should follow the C's example and set aside some time for quiet introspection while the C works on opening up and sharing his or her inner world. Another strategy would be for the A to help the C become more sensual and hedonistic, with the C showing the A more effective time-management techniques so that the demands of your life together can be better handled.

As for the problem with your differing social needs, the A will need to stop pushing the C to get more involved in social activities. This will result in the C withdrawing even more, from the A as well as the A's friends and acquaintances. The A should make it clear that the C is welcome to join him or her in socializing but not pass judgment or use pressure to get the C to become more social. Instead, the A can curtail his or her socializing just a little so you can spend some time together with just the two of you. The C is then more likely to reciprocate by agreeing to spend more time doing the things that the A likes to do.

Also work hard to understand each other. Rather than the C becoming furious with the A for being so easygoing and accusing the A of not caring enough to get involved in heated arguments, the C needs to realize that the A simply doesn't enjoy confrontations and will do anything to avoid them. But it doesn't mean that the A doesn't care. In actuality, the A cares deeply about people in general and his or her partner in particular. Recognizing the other person's needs as they relate to his or her behavioral patterns will go a long way in dealing with your differences.

B	B		4

A dual-B relationship is filled with excitement. Both of you are active, adventurous types who are happiest when challenging yourselves to reach new goals. Other types of partners might not understand why you find it so important to continually explore new horizons and expand your personal abilities, but one B completely identifies with another B's needs in this area. You'll encourage each other to realize your fullest potential, not through words but by your own examples. You'll also feed off each other's love of travel and find yourselves going places that would be off limits in any other relationship.

A double-B couple is often perceived as having it all. Not only are you involved in more intriguing leisure activities than most couples, but you also do better in the work world. You both are natural leaders, full of ambition and determination to succeed. It's no wonder that B's quickly rise to the top in their fields. Any B is going to do well, but a relationship with another B will inspire him or her to attain even greater heights. Your success will enable you to live exactly as you want. A B-B couple will usually have more material possessions and luxury items than other couples, but no one could begrudge you for it because you've earned it.

Is yours an ideal relationship? Actually, no. It has its share of flaws just like other pairings. For one thing, the leadership ability you share leads to a great deal of competition. Neither one of you likes to give up control. You'll run into trouble in situations where there can be only one leader. Since you both are unwilling to relinquish power, you'll fight to hold on to it. In fact, fighting will be a frequent occurrence in your relationship. Unlike other types who shy away from confrontation, you B types enjoy it. You like the adrenaline rush you get as you spar against each other, both determined to be the victor.

Arguments also occur because of your limited communication. You don't express yourself well with words, so you tend to avoid discussing important issues and topics. As a result, you may not understand each other as well as you should. Misunderstandings are never really resolved, and you can even begin to lose touch with each other's feelings and thoughts. Your individual lives may be exciting and fulfilling, but you may stop connecting together as a couple.

Your high activity involvement keeps you busy and stimulated. You're never at a loss for something to do. Boredom is not a problem in your relationship. However, even a B has only a finite amount of energy and time at his or her disposal. It may be that you're putting more effort into other things (e.g., clubs, associations, exercise, or hobbies) than your relationship. No coupling can really prosper under these conditions, so try to devote more time and attention to each other.

B C	5

You're very good for each other in every possible way. You balance each other well, adding what the other lacks and giving you a wholeness as a couple that you lack as individuals. You fall on opposite extremes on the dichotomy of body versus mind. The B tends to neglect his or her mental processes in favor of corporal pursuits. Thus, while the B is as physically fit as anyone could ever hope to be, he or she will seldom challenge his or her mind in any way. The C, on the other hand, is totally cerebral and emphasizes thoughts rather than feeling or action. The C is typically so busy contemplating what to do that she or he never does anything other than think. With the influence of a B, the C will be compelled to start taking action and make dreams happen. The C in turn will help the B realize that true health and fitness combine the intellectual and physical aspects, leading the B to develop his or her neglected brain power.

The C is a very private individual who needs regular doses of time alone. No matter how involved the C is in a relationship, he or she has to have time to escape into his or her private inner world.

Other types are so insecure and dependent that they'd feel threatened and unhappy by this need of the C. But the B is perfectly content to accommodate the C and actually prefers for you both to lead your own lives some of the time. Since the B has so many resources and outlets of his or her own, many of which are of no interest to the C, it works well for both of you to pursue your own things. Just make sure to reserve some time for each other.

The partner who gains the most from this relationship is the C. The B helps round out the C personality in several ways. For one thing, the B is very adventurous and fearless while the C tends to tread cautiously through life. Without a B in the picture, the apprehensive C can become so inhibited by doubt and fear as to miss out on many experiences that promise to be enriching (albeit just a little risky). The C also tends to be given to intense but short bursts of energy. This fluctuating energy cycle typically results in the C's starting many projects but never finishing them. The B, having a more even temperament and work pace, will ensure that all necessary activities are completed. But don't think this relationship is one-sided. The B's personality is enhanced by several of the C's traits, including that of sensitivity. The C may be a loner but has an acute awareness of other people's moods and needs, whereas the B tends to be oblivious to such things. A relationship with a C helps the B become more empathetic and, ultimately, more caring.

C C	3

Because C's are such unique individuals, a double-C relationship is a special one that is entirely different from any other. You both have well-developed intellectual abilities and can provide each other with the mental stimulation you thrive on. Other partners may feel that a C is just too brainy, but one C appreciates another and does everything possible to enhance his or her own intellectual prowess as well as that of his or her partner. You both enjoy learning new things and will support each other in acquiring new skills and ideas. Growth is most important to a dual-C couple. You'll expend large amounts of energy in making sure you don't become stagnant mentally.

While maximizing your intellectual potential is of the utmost concern, your physical fitness is apt to be neglected. Even if everyone else is busy working out or engaging in some physical activity of their choice, C's will tend to avoid joining them, particularly if there's some activity available that would provide intellectual stimulation (e.g., a good book, music, or educational television). With today's emphasis on physical fitness, those who aren't very concerned with developing their bodies are perceived as being different and even a little weird. But this doesn't bother a double-C couple because you have each other for moral support.

Similarly, your emotional sides are likely to be underemphasized as well. Being able to express your feelings isn't important to either of you; all that you care about is the ability to express your thoughts, and you both are experts at that. You'll communicate with each other about your daily lives and the world at large, but you'll never quite be able to share your emotions with each other. This usually doesn't present any problems since neither of you wants intense emotional displays. Occasionally, however, one of you may find that you've totally misunderstood what the other person was feeling. This will be through no fault of your own since your partner never made his or her feelings clear, but it can lead to hurt, resentment, and confusion between you.

Both of you are private people who often need to be by yourselves to recharge your personal batteries. As a couple, you won't cultivate a large circle of acquaintances or experience a very full social life. But this suits two C's just fine. You'll have a few close friends but neither of you will force the other to partake in social activities. Nobody can appreciate the need for solitude and quiet reflection better than a fellow C.

But even with your empathetic understanding and acceptance of each other, there will still be quite a few problems in your relationship. All too often, you'll feel that the other has insulted or betrayed you in some way and furious arguments will follow. You'll tend to not finish all the details and necessities in your life together because you have short bursts of energy that you can't sustain for the length of time needed to complete certain projects. You share a proclivity for becoming extremely stressed out and no matter how hard you try, you may only add to the other person's tensions. But chances are that you'll view these merely as the price you have to pay for being with someone so intellectually dynamic and exciting; neither one of you will ever want to end the relationship, regardless of any problems you encounter.

Eye Color

Some scientists are convinced that specific personality traits are linked to certain eye colors. They believe that the color of pigments in the eye affects different areas in the brain, thus influencing behavior. For example, dark-eyed individuals tend to react more quickly and intensely to stimuli than their lighter-eyed counterparts.

Eye color may play a partial role in how you relate to each other. Find the color pair that best describes the two of you and learn about the strengths and weaknesses associated with your color combination.

Person 1	Eye color	Person 2
_____	Blue/gray	_____
_____	Dark brown/black	_____
_____	Green/hazel	_____
_____	Light brown	_____

| BLUE/GRAY | BLUE/GRAY | 4 |

Your relationship has its problems, but you both have the patience and determination to find solutions to most of them. Stubbornness is a mutual characteristic, but this isn't necessarily negative. You refuse to give up even in the roughest of times and this can result in your staying together when other couples would have split up. Your tenacity can enable both of you to eventually get what you want, provided you work hard to achieve it.

Yours can be the type of relationship other couples envy. You both have a wonderful capacity for being sentimental, complete with all the trimmings (such as flowers, candlelight, and champagne) for special occasions. When you take the time to appreciate each other, you can have a fairy-tale romance. Unfortunately, the two of you often get bogged down by your daily routine and then wonder why there doesn't seem to be as many sparks as there used to be in your relationship.

One of the best-kept secrets is that people with blue or gray eyes can be quite moody. Your dark-eyed peers may show it more visibly, but you can experience as many emotional highs and lows. Respect each other's rights to privacy and understanding during these trying times. Be sure to treat your partner the way you'd want to be treated yourself, since you both tend to hold a grudge when you believe you've been mistreated.

| BLUE/GRAY | DARK BROWN/BLACK | 3 |

You're likely to experience significant ups and downs in your relationship. A blue/gray-dark brown/black pairing rarely remains on an even keel. Both of you can be more than a little hot-tempered. Whereas the dark brown/black tends to react immediately, the blue/gray does a slow simmer and eventually explodes. Either way, both are apt to say things that will later be regretted. Your relationship can become an endless cycle of fighting, making up, and then fighting all over again. If you're determined to make this volatile pairing work, be sure to air your differences before resentment builds and emotions get out of control. Schedule regular discussions in which you calmly resolve the inevitable conflicts that occur when two strong personalities are romantically involved.

Each of you brings a unique perspective to the relationship. The dark brown/black-eyed person tends to crave action and adventure while the blue/gray-eyed individual feels most comfortable in stable, familiar environments. If you each make an effort to accept the other's needs, you should be able to coexist harmoniously. The tranquillity that the blue/gray seeks can be enjoyed by the dark brown/black as an occasional relief from the hectic pursuit of exciting experiences. The dark brown/black-eyed partner can help the blue/gray escape from the rut she or he is likely to fall into, adding a new lift to what could otherwise be a boring existence. The blue/gray and dark brown/black can each add something quite special to the other person's life.

BLUE/GRAY	**GREEN/HAZEL**	**4**

Your relationship has some definite strengths and weaknesses. The green/hazel-eyed partner can be a very positive influence on his or her blue/gray-eyed counterpart. The emotional stability of the green/hazel effectively balances the blue/gray's moodiness. Mood swings are unavoidable to some extent in a blue/gray-eyed person, but they tend to be less severe when there's a green/hazel-eyed romantic interest. The green/hazel's even-natured temperament typically inspires the blue to strive for a similarly calm outlook and manner.

In a blue/gray-green/hazel relationship, there is always the risk of the more determined blue/gray taking advantage of the somewhat passive green/hazel. But this usually doesn't happen if the blue/gray is careful not to take the green/hazel-eyed partner for granted. It is important that the green/hazel's loyalty and integrity be fully appreciated. Fortunately, the very romantic blue/gray has no difficulty demonstrating affection and can let the green/hazel know how much she or he is cherished. Show each other the consideration you both deserve, and your relationship can last a lifetime.

BLUE/GRAY	LIGHT BROWN	4

The two of you share a major personality characteristic, determination. You each know exactly what you want and are willing to do whatever it takes to get it. Once you form an opinion or set a goal, there's no turning back. Neither one is big on compromise. It's all or nothing, and both the blue/gray-light brown want it all . . . their own ways. This isn't a problem when you have the same desires or plans, but it can become a major obstacle to a continuing, satisfying relationship when the blue/gray and light brown want different things. If you want your relationship to last, you both will need to learn how to compromise and negotiate win-win strategies.

The blue/gray and light brown can help to balance each other's strong character traits. The very traditional blue/gray can become a little more relaxed and creative through association with the less conventional light brown. The light brown, on the other hand, can benefit from the blue/gray's steady, meticulous ways, becoming less scattered and better organized. Whenever possible, try to capitalize on your individual strengths. For example, the logical, orderly blue/gray can concentrate on the details and necessities, while the flighty, fanciful light brown brings fun and excitement into your lives. With a little effort, this relationship can enjoy the best of both personality types.

DARK BROWN/BLACK	DARK BROWN/BLACK	1

It's highly unlikely that your relationship will ever be dull. Both of you are full of passion, throwing yourselves completely into everything you do. Observing life from the sidelines is not your style; you make sure you're actively participating in all that life can offer. This drive and energy enables you to enjoy more adventure and excitement together than most couples can ever hope to have. The time you spend in each other's company is far from boring. Your relationship can remain stimulating no matter how long you've been together.

While your passionate natures generate a special chemistry between the two of you, it can cause substantial problems as well. Controlling your tempers can be difficult, if not impossible. Arguments tend to be a frequent occurrence. Unlike other couples who can peacefully discuss their disagreements, you usually overreact and quickly find yourselves in a shouting match. If your relationship is going to survive, you'll need to learn to relax and not take things so seriously. The little things really aren't worth fighting about and the bigger issues can only be resolved in a calm, rational manner. Make every effort to fight fairly when you do quarrel, avoiding personal attacks on each other.

| DARK BROWN/BLACK | GREEN/HAZEL | 5 |

Consider yourselves fortunate if you're a dark brown/black-green/hazel couple. This relationship can be totally fulfilling for both partners. The green/hazel and dark brown/black bring out the best in each other. While the dark brown/black-eyed partner sizzles with intensity, the green/hazel-eyed partner provides a more mellow perspective. When both individuals are open to learning from each other, the green/hazel can acquire a heightened zest for living, and the dark brown/black can develop a calmer approach to life, decreasing his or her chances of burning out on the job or at home. The sense of excitement that the dark brown/black brings to the relationship can be enjoyed by both partners, but the green/hazel's influence tames it to the point where it doesn't get out of hand.

The only couple that communicates better is a double green/hazel pair. Dark brown/black-green/hazel couples have a remarkable ability to share their innermost thoughts and feelings with each other. The unrestrained dark brown/black typically doesn't hold back under most circumstances and this is especially the case when she or he has a green/hazel-eyed partner. The green/hazel's caring and sincerity encourages open discussion. The dark brown/black, in turn, respects the green/hazel's giving nature and tries to reciprocate as much as possible.

DARK BROWN/BLACK	**LIGHT BROWN**	3

Yours is a highly charged relationship. Expect it to be always stimulating and unpredictable. The dynamic natures of both partners ensures that the relationship will never become stagnant. New experiences and exotic adventures continually broaden your horizons, both as individuals and as a couple. It's unlikely that the dark brown/black and light brown would ever lose interest in each other. You each make sure that life is filled with fun and excitement. You're both convinced that the world offers many possibilities and are determined to take full advantage of them.

At their best, dark brown/black-light brown relationships are wonderful, but they also have the potential to be disastrous. Both of you have a tendency to be fiercely competitive and may unconsciously try to upstage each other. Instead of being mutually supportive, the dark brown/black and light brown each vies to be the center of attention. When not carried to extremes, this can be challenging, but it can easily get out of hand. Both partners in a dark brown/black-light brown relationship need to make sure that they protect their friendship and not become rivals or adversaries. Try to remember that you're a team working together to build a relationship that enables both your egos to be stroked.

GREEN/HAZEL	**GREEN/HAZEL**	5

You have the potential for a warmly loving relationship full of mutual respect and admiration. Both of you have a great deal of empathy and can readily identify with the other's feelings. Your understanding natures and good listening skills facilitate communication. Secrets are rare; you usually confide in each other to a far greater extent than most couples. You know you can count on the other to be fair and just. Your relationship is characterized by complete trust and integrity.

There aren't many things that can go wrong in a double-green/hazel relationship, but you do need to be careful not to get so wrapped up in each other that you lose your individual selves. It's important that each of you retain your unique individuality. You also need to make sure that you cultivate other relationships and interests. While it's understandable that you want to spend as much time together as possible, this should not be at the expense of separate friendships. Expand your social horizons to include a variety of people and experiences.

GREEN/HAZEL	LIGHT BROWN	4

A green/hazel-light brown relationship enables both partners to grow and reach their ultimate potentials. The green/hazel excels at providing the emotional security that encourages the light brown to realize his or her special promise. Knowing that the green/hazel can be counted on for unconditional support, the light brown feels free to explore and experiment. The green/hazel partner, on the other hand, is not by nature an adventurer, but exposure to the light brown's free-spirited ways will probably lead to an increased willingness to take risks and make changes. With a partner of a different eye color, the green/hazel can become somewhat stagnant, but a light brown partner will facilitate growth.

If you're a green/hazel-light brown couple, you already know how fulfilling this relationship can be for both partners. The only potential danger can be differing expectations for your relationship. The green/hazel is very much couple-oriented and feels complete only as part of a pair. The light brown is more of a loner and can feel smothered if not given enough space. This is not to say that the light brown is incapable of making a commitment, but she or he needs more freedom and solitude than does the green/hazel. If the green/hazel-eyed partner can learn to accept this and not feel betrayed by the light brown's independence, there should be no difficulty in maintaining a long-term relationship.

| LIGHT BROWN | LIGHT BROWN | 2 |

Although the two of you share the same eye color, you're far from being identical twins. Highly individualistic, you each know exactly who you are and are true to your own selves. Nonconformity is the one character trait you have in common. You both cultivate your own personal styles, leading others to view you as one of the most interesting couples around.

Your differences and refusal to lose your own identities helps to keep your relationship fresh and exciting. On a more negative note, however, these same characteristics can interfere with your ability to blend together and form a true union. You tend to function as two separate individuals who live/work/play side by side rather than as an interdependent pair whose whole is greater than the sum of its parts. Try to make sure that you share significant parts of your life together as opposed to experiencing adjacent lives that just happen to intersect on a haphazard basis. You can still retain your individuality while learning from and growing with the other.

Hands

The study of palmistry focuses on the meanings of the lines and markings in the palms of human hands. There are three major lines (life, head, and heart) that are found in every hand and reveal many interesting character traits about the owner of the particular hands in question. By analyzing your own hands and then comparing them with your partner's, you may be able to learn a great deal about how you relate to each other.

The three major lines are readily visible and may be studied just by observing them in your palms. However, it may help to dust the palm with white powder or flour to make them even easier to read. A magnifying glass can provide further assistance. It's also possible to make handprints so that you can conveniently study and compare your hands. This then provides a permanent record and will enable you to use other books and resources to study the lines and markings in more depth if you so desire.

To make a handprint, spread water-soluble block-printer's ink in your palm. Note that right-handed people will probably want to study their left hands, and vice versa for lefties. Wait until the ink is nearly dry, then press your hand on plain white paper, making sure to press all the curves and depressions of the palm onto the paper.

Life Line

Contrary to popular belief, the life line does not reveal the length of people's lives or the time of their deaths. Instead, it depicts their overall vitality and involvement in life. Look at the illustration to learn what a standard life line looks like. It should be strong and clear, encircling the entire thumb and continuing down to the wrist. If this describes your life line, you can consider yourself to have a standard type. However, many people's life lines deviate to some extent from the standard. After reading about the other varieties of life lines, select the one that best describes each of yours and then compare your answers.

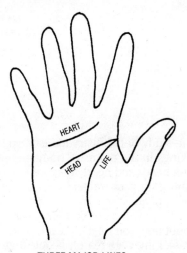

THREE MAJOR LINES

Deep life line: very noticeably etched into the hand
Weak life line: barely visible
Mount of Jupiter life line: begins closer to the base of the index
    finger than the thumb
Mount of Neptune life line: ends on the wrist, but far away from
    the thumb or even the index finger . . . ends underneath the
    little finger
Forked life line: two or more branches at the beginning (by the
    thumb) merging into the main line

Split or broken life line: branches off from the beginning of the thumb and ending in two or more different spots on the wrist or stopping at some point and then starting again
Short life line: never reaching the base of the palm
Joined life line: life, head, and heart lines are joined at the beginning

Which type of life line do each of you have?

Person 1	Type	Person 2
_____	Standard	_____
_____	Deep	_____
_____	Weak	_____
_____	Jupiter	_____
_____	Neptune	_____
_____	Forked	_____
_____	Split/broken	_____
_____	Short	_____
_____	Joined	_____

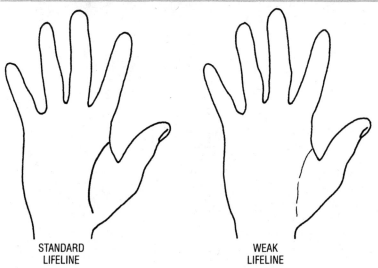

STANDARD
LIFELINE

WEAK
LIFELINE

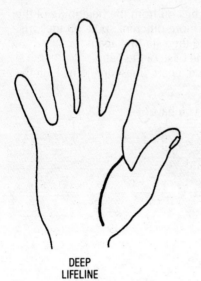

**DEEP
LIFELINE**

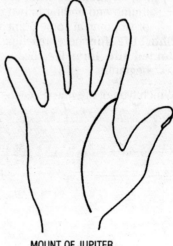

**MOUNT OF JUPITER
LIFELINE**

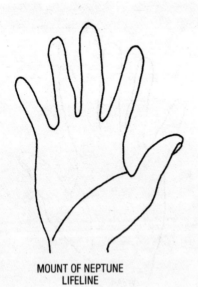

**MOUNT OF NEPTUNE
LIFELINE**

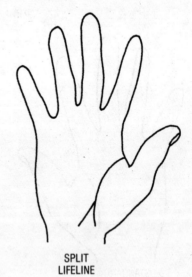

**SPLIT
LIFELINE**

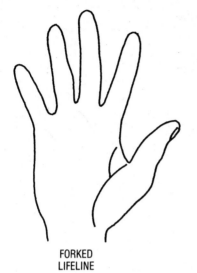

FORKED
LIFELINE

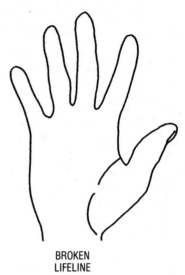

BROKEN
LIFELINE

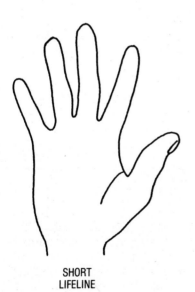

SHORT
LIFELINE

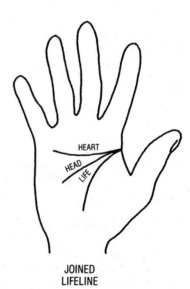

JOINED
LIFELINE

| | |
| STANDARD   STANDARD | 5 |

You two share a healthy outlook on life. You both like to be active and busy, but you know how to relax as well.

| | |
| STANDARD   DEEP | 3 |

The standard-lined partner can keep up with the deep-liner but may become exhausted in doing so. The deep-lined partner always wants to be doing something and never wants to do it only halfway. This can be exciting at first to the standard-lined partner but can eventually lead to him or her burning out and retreating from the deep's excesses.

| | |
| STANDARD   WEAK | 4 |

The standard-lined partner can help the weak-liner become more involved in life. By gradually exposing the weak-lined partner to new experiences and encouraging him or her to partake, the standard-liner can be an excellent role model. If the standard-lined partner has the patience to deal with the weak's reticence and the weak-lined partner can trust the standard-liner enough to take some risks, your coupling can succeed.

| | |
| STANDARD   JUPITER | 3 |

There will be some friction in your relationship, but you should be able to work through it. The Jupiter-lined partner always wants to lead although the standard-liner is often reluctant to follow. The standard-liner has a mind of his or her own and can't be as passive as the Jupiter-liner would like. The Jupiter-lined partner will need to relinquish his or her leadership role in favor of an equal partnership so that the standard-liner can be happy.

STANDARD	NEPTUNE	4

The Neptune-lined partner will find fascinating adventures for you both to enjoy. You'll find a great deal of pleasure experimenting with new people, places, and ideas. The only potential problem is that the standard-liner likes to establish some roots, whereas the Neptunian has a constant case of wanderlust. You'll have to learn to compromise so that both your needs can be satisfied.

STANDARD	FORKED	5

You two are perfectly matched. Both of you want to get a lot out of life, but never in a reckless manner. You're supportive of each other and can cope with any changes that your life together may experience.

STANDARD	SPLIT/BROKEN	2

The standard-lined partner has a lot of spunk, but even he or she may be unprepared for the turbulence that a split-liner will bring into his or her life. If you stay together, you'll need to develop some strategies for dealing with the stress of having your lives frequently and dramatically change because of the split-lined partner's erratic behavior and impulsive decisions.

STANDARD	SHORT	1

The joie de vivre of the standard-lined partner can be helpful for the listless short-liner. But the standard-liner can't be expected to change the short-liner completely by him- or herself; some of the motivation and energy for enjoying life has to come from the short-liner. The short-liner may have more than his or her fair share of health concerns and complaints but should still make the effort to develop a more positive attitude for the sake of the well-adjusted standard-liner.

STANDARD	JOINED	4

You'll have an exciting life together, but the joined-lined partner may get you both into disastrous situations. Fortunately, the standard-liner has the ability to carefully think things out and use good judgment. If the standard-liner is firm about not participating in things that have the potential to be dangerous, the two of you should be quite happy together.

DEEP	DEEP	4

Of all the possible pairings, a couple who are both deep-lined are the ones who will have the most active and interesting lives. There is no end to your combined energy and spirit. You're both ready for whatever challenges life offers. You can share a life together that other couples can only dream about. But there is one drawback to this unrestrained relationship. You'll tend to sacrifice warmth and communication in the midst of nonstop racing to do and achieve everything you desire.

| DEEP | WEAK | | 1 |

Each of you is the complete opposite of the other. The weak-lined partner is more than satisfied to watch from the sidelines, whereas the deep has to be in the forefront of whatever is going on. Obviously it isn't easy to merge the deep's action-packed life-style with the weak-liner's preference for low-key living. You'll each need to have some separate areas of your lives that the other person isn't part of. But this needn't prevent you from enjoying each other during the time you reserve to share your lives and yourselves.

| DEEP | JUPITER | | 4 |

You share the same ambitious, action-oriented natures. You'll generally have a fulfulling relationship together. However, there will be times when you become overly competitive with each other and lose sight of what you should be striving for: becoming the most supportive, loving partners each of you can be. Take some time out from your busy schedules and discuss your deepest feelings. Remind yourselves that there is enough ruthlessness in this world; your relationship needs compassion, caring, and honesty.

| DEEP | NEPTUNE | | 5 |

No problems here. Neither of you is a conformist; you both enjoy experimenting with unorthodox things. Whatever one of you wants to try, the other will have an open mind and won't stand in the way. You both are secure enough to leave the old ways behind and experience something new.

| DEEP | FORKED | 5 |

The forked-lined individual can lead a satisfying life on his or her own, but things will be even better with a deep-lined partner. Although somewhat quieter and slightly more cautious, the forked-liner can still be a worthwhile companion for the deep-liner. You both have a zest for living that will enable you to realize your full potential and be the type of people you each want to be.

| DEEP | SPLIT/BROKEN | 4 |

Life is never predictable with a split/broken-lined partner, but this shouldn't be a problem for the deep-lined individual. The deep-liner thrives on adventure and new experiences, so she or he should be able to take in stride the changes that accompany a split/broken-liner's life-style. Both of you should strive to develop some routines and rituals, however, since this can add a sense of balance to your relationship. You'll feel more like you can count on each other if you have some things that remain constant in your daily lives.

| DEEP | SHORT | 1 |

Your pairing has a proclivity for emotional distance. Because the short-liner lacks the energy to keep up with the deep-liner, the deep-lined partner may focus his or her attention on other people or things. If this happens, the short-lined individual will feel abandoned when what he or she needs most is support and comfort. To avoid becoming more like strangers than friends and lovers, set aside time to communicate your feelings. Even if the other person disappoints you at times, always relate to him or her in an open, caring, gentle manner.

| DEEP   JOINED | 2 |

Be very careful with this relationship. The two of you are apt to be so involved in living to the hilt that you might not be aware that you've made some impulsive decisions and acted in ways that could destroy your union. Learn to say no to things that could be detrimental to your love and trust. You can still have full lives without partaking in everything available; some experiences and people are best avoided.

| WEAK   WEAK | 1 |

Unless you make a gigantic effort to put some excitement and challenge in your lives, you'll have less than a stimulating relationship. Make sure you're not staying together simply because it takes too much effort to find other partners. Help your relationship become more rewarding in its own right. Push yourselves to become more involved in life and you'll have more to share with each other.

| WEAK   JUPITER | 5 |

While a Jupiter–weak-lined coupling should be beneficial to both of you, it is most helpful to the weak-lined partner. She or he can be motivated by the ambitious Jupiter partner to become more engaged in life. The weak-liner won't be able to put off making decisions or setting goals when a dynamic Jupiter is in the picture. This relationship can be advantageous to the Jupiter partner as well, since the weak-lined individual won't add any demands or pressures to the Jupiter's life.

WEAK	NEPTUNE	3

Your relationship could go either way. It could work out well if the Neptune is able to inspire the weak-lined partner to participate more in life and take a few chances. If the weak-liner can be persuaded to travel and experience different life-styles, you may be able to live together in a harmonious manner. But if the weak-lined person is determined to maintain his or her lackluster existence, the Neptune will likely move on to a more compatible partner.

WEAK	FORKED	5

A forked-line partner is one of the best choices for a weak-lined individual. With a forked-line person in his or her life, the weak-liner can't help but become more active and involved. The forked-line partner adds the enthusiasm and vitality that is totally missing in a weak-lined person. Gradually, the weak-liner will engage in a variety of experiences that she or he would have missed if not for the example set by the forked-liner. Other people might get discouraged or tired if they continually had to coax a weak-lined partner to start living rather than just existing, but a forked-lined individual's boundless energy will enable him or her to do whatever it takes to get the reticent partner to lead a full life.

WEAK	SPLIT/BROKEN	1

Yours is a difficult relationship. The weak-liner usually lacks the stamina to deal with all the changes that the split/broken-liner will bring into your lives. The turbulent life of the split/broken-lined individual requires a partner who can cope with whatever comes along. For both your sakes, work toward helping the weak-lined partner develop more mental and physical energy. This is helpful for the split/broken-liner as well since she or he needs to have a positive attitude and healthy body to deal with all the challenges of life.

| WEAK   SHORT | 1 |

Take care to ensure that this relationship doesn't become draining for either of you. The short-lined individual will frequently deplete the weak-liner's limited energy reserves. The weak-liner will have difficulty fully leading his or her own life, much less providing all the needed care for someone as physically and/ or emotionally fragile as the short-liner. For your union to survive, you both must make a maximum effort to develop the strength you need to get through life. Also establish a supportive network of friends and family who can help you cope when things get rough.

| WEAK   JOINED | 5 |

As unlikely as it may seem since you're so different, your relationship can work out for both of you. The weak-lined partner's natural reticence can be just the safety mechanism that the joined-lined individual needs. The impulsive and reckless daring of the joined-liner can be tempered by the weak-lined person's refusal to get involved in dangerous escapades. But the joined-lined partner can never be completely subdued and can inspire the weak-liner to enjoy a little more spontaneity and risk-taking in his or her life.

| JUPITER   JUPITER | 1 |

Trouble won't be uncommon in your relationship. You both tend to be extremely competitive and you'll often find that because each of you is so determined to win, regardless of the consequences, you'll even be willing to hurt each other in the process of getting what you want. Both of you lack patience and tolerance, so you'll have to endure many fights if you stay together.

JUPITER	NEPTUNE	4

A Neptunian partner can be like a breath of fresh air for the Jupiter. The Neptune individual's main priority is to enjoy life by exploring the world, whereas the Jupiter tends to place all his or her energy into work. Under the guidance of the Neptune, the Jupiter may begin to get involved in other activities outside of the work world. The Jupiter, once plied away from his or her desk, can be an enthusiastic traveling companion for the Neptune.

JUPITER	FORKED	5

The two of you should have a joyful relationship. Your shared life will be full of activity because you both are always ready to tackle new challenges. The vivacious forked-lined personality needs a dynamic partner; the Jupiter fits this description perfectly. The Jupiter does best with someone who is strong enough to be an equal partner but without being competitive or aggressive, and the forked-liner is able to provide just this sort of companionship. Without a doubt, you'll enjoy every moment that you spend together.

JUPITER	SPLIT/BROKEN	5

Dealing with the unpredictable and ever-changing split/broken-lined personality is a formidable task, but the Jupiter is one of the few individuals who is up to the challenge. The Jupiter's confidence, decision-making ability, and coping skills make it possible for him or her to take charge of any situation. Split/broken-lined individuals who are involved with a Jupiter partner should consider themselves very fortunate indeed.

JUPITER	SHORT	1

To avoid the Jupiter individual's perception of being tied down by the short-lined partner, the short-liner has two choices: either develop the get-up-and-go needed for keeping up with a Jupiter partner or make sure that the Jupiter is given enough freedom to actively pursue his or her life without being restricted by the short-liner. The short-liner needs to realize that a partner as dynamic and special as the Jupiter is well worth the effort of making some changes.

JUPITER	JOINED	5

One of the most notable traits of a Jupiter-lined person is excellent decision-making ability. This comes in handy with a joined-lined partner, since this individual is notorious for acting rashly and often unwisely. A Jupiter partner can make sure that you both stay out of dangerous or compromising situations.

NEPTUNE	NEPTUNE	5

What more could a Neptunian want than another Neptunian? The two of you are guaranteed to have an incredibly exciting life together. You share the same love of travel, hating to be tied down to any locale that becomes too familiar. Other people would be unnerved by a Neptunian's desire to continually be on the move, but one Neptune can understand another's needs. Your life-style is apt to be fairly unconventional, but that should suit each of you very well.

NPETUNE   FORKED   5

Yours is a great combination. The forked-line individual has a love of life that blends nicely with the Neptunian's adventurous spirit. Together you can travel the globe and share varied experiences. You should be very happy with each other.

NEPTUNE   SPLIT/BROKEN   2

A Neptune individual has the necessary fortitude for dealing with the ups and downs of life with a split/broken-lined partner. However, he or she is often too busy pursuing his or her own interests to fully address the varying needs of the split/broken-lined partner. Resentment can occur if the split/broken-liner feels neglected or if the Neptunian has to continually revise his or her plans to suit the split/broken-liner. To avoid these negative feelings and their impact on your relationship, you both must be as considerate of each other as possible. Take the other person's feelings into account and respect his or her unique needs.

NEPTUNE   SHORT   1

Your relationship can succeed only if the short-lined partner can become more independent. The Neptunian cannot be happy with a partner who ties him or her down. Therefore, the short-liner must become less needy or learn to satisfy his or her needs through other people or things. It's not that the Neptune partner doesn't care; he or she does but can't devote all his or her time and energy to just one person to the exclusion of everything else. If the short-liner can learn to function as the Neptune's equal rather than as his or her dependent, you'll both prosper in the relationship.

NEPTUNE	JOINED	5

The two of you may get into some situations that will cause your adrenaline to skyrocket, but this will make you feel alive. Both Neptune and joined-lined individuals need a rush of excitement on a regular basis. Neither one of you is interested in making informed, conservative decisions; you both prefer to act on your impulses and deal with the consequences later. Your reckless life-style wouldn't work for most couples, but it's right for you two.

FORKED	FORKED	5

A dual-forked-lined couple truly has it all. You share high levels of vitality and self-confidence, enabling you to try to succeed in a great variety of experiences. You're capable of leading busy individual lives while still finding time for each other. You enjoy excellent communication together because you both have open minds and tolerant attitudes. You're one of those rare combinations in which everything is absolutely perfect.

FORKED	SPLIT/BROKEN	4

A split/broken-lined individual will inevitably bring many surprises into your shared life and not all of them will be desirable. But because the forked-liner has excellent mental health, she or he can deal with whatever life brings. The forked-lined individual may have more fun with a different partner, but the two of you can work things out if you choose to be together.

FORKED	SHORT	3

The forked-line individual has a well-rounded personality and one of his or her most outstanding traits is being highly compassionate. Realizing that the short-liner lacks energy and determination, the forked-lined partner will make every effort to improve life for his or her needy counterpart. Whenever possible, the forked-liner will accommodate his or her partner. But the forked-liner is not a saint and there *are* limits to his or her benevolence. To prevent the forked-lined partner from feeling taken advantage of, the short-liner must be careful not to make excessive demands. If the short-liner tries to give as well as take, both of you can be happy in the relationship.

FORKED	JOINED	4

You should do well with each other. Although the joined-lined partner can be exasperating at times because of his or her tendency to rush fearlessly into situations without considering the advisability of such actions, the forked-liner will be able to keep the joined-liner in control. The forked-lined partner enjoys new experiences just as much as the joined-liner but will use better judgment and keep you both out of trouble. The two of you should have a full, exciting, but (thanks to the forked-liner) relatively safe, life together.

SPLIT/BROKEN	SPLIT/BROKEN	1

A split/broken-lined person's life is usually full of turmoil. When two split/broken-lined individuals share a life, the result may be a total disruption of any sort of stable life-style. Fortunately, you both prefer being in flux to being stagnant. But you do need to give considerable thought to any changes *before* you make them. Change in healthy doses can be challenging and growth-promoting, but an excessive amount or the wrong choices can be disastrous. If you can proactively analyze every situation instead of impulsively reacting to it, your lives and your relationship will be less stressful.

SPLIT/BROKEN	SHORT	1

Be prepared for some trying times in this relationship. The split/broken-lined individual is very involved with his or her own life and will have difficulty dealing with the dependency of a short-lined partner. The short-liner will be hurt by the lack of attention and may even feel unloved. Each of you needs to increase your understanding of the other. The split/broken-liner must realize that the short-liner hasn't been so blessed with energy and determination as has a split/broken-lined individual. Coping with problems will always be more difficult for the short-lined partner and the split/broken-liner must be sympathetic to this. But this doesn't absolve the short-liner of any responsibility. To the contrary, the short-liner must learn to become less clinging and more able to stand on his or her own two feet. Your relationship will improve if you each change your perspectives.

SPLIT/BROKEN	JOINED	5

Yours is a very compatible combination. You share many of the same traits: you're both daring, enjoy taking risks, and aren't happy in a stable, predictable life-style. Your life together will undergo many changes and variations, but neither of you would really want it any other way. At times you may experience emotional discomfort or pain because of the choices you've made, but that's the price of constant experimentation. Just make sure to share as many aspects of your turbulent lives with each other as possible so you'll remain a connected couple.

| SHORT | SHORT | 1 |

A dual-short-lined couple is apt to have a comfortable but lackluster relationship unless you develop strategies for overcoming your mutual lack of self-confidence and vigor. Make a promise right now to each other that you'll begin a self-improvement program to maximize your abilities and zest for living. If you both can become stronger and more capable in your own rights, you'll each have more to bring to the relationship.

| SHORT | JOINED | 1 |

There's a significant potential for difficulty in your relationship. The short-lined partner tends to have some trouble coping with life and the disaster-prone joined-liner can easily add to these troubles. Rather than helping the short-liner resolve his or her problems, the joined-lined partner is likely to be so wrapped up in his or her own precarious life situation as to forget about the needs of the short-liner. If you allow this to happen, you'll grow away from each other and will lose your feelings of commitment to the relationship. To prevent this from occurring, you each need to look beyond your individual selves and your immediate problems. Concern yourselves instead with the needs of the other person. Help resolve his problems and you'll go a long way toward improving your closeness and communication.

| JOINED | JOINED | 1 |

When two joined-liners become romantically attached, there will be a tendency to accentuate your mutual impulsivity. As a result, you'll continually find yourselves in trouble that could have been avoided if a more thoughtful approach were taken. This proclivity toward reckless behavior can wreak havoc with your lives and interfere with a stable relationship. For the sake of your individual safety as well as for your stability as a couple, it's imperative that you both learn to contemplate the consequences before you take any action. Before you make decisions of any significance, consider all your options, discuss their advantages and disadvantages, and mutually arrive at the most rational conclusion.

Head Line

The head or mind line reveals the way a person thinks. The standard head line is clearly visible and connects with the life line, beginning at the index finger and ending at the ring finger. It typically runs into the center of the palm.

Look at your palm and determine whether you each have a standard head line or one of the other varieties described below. Then compare your types of head lines to learn what they say about the compatibility of your intellectual styles.

Separated head line: begins above the life line without connecting

Short head line: stops at the center of the palm, under the middle finger (instead of the ring finger)

Curved/Neptune head line: curves significantly downward and ends above the wrist directly under the little finger

Straight head line: runs straight across the palm, close to the heart line, and ends right below the base of the little finger

Split head line: divides into two before it reaches the center of the palm

Branched head line: ending in two or more branches and possibly going into different directions

Joined head line: continues to be joined to the life line past the index finger and may be connected to the heart line as well

Broken head line: actually stops at some point and then begins again

Weak head line: is barely visible

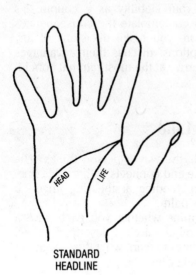

STANDARD
HEADLINE

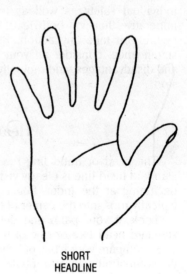

SHORT
HEADLINE

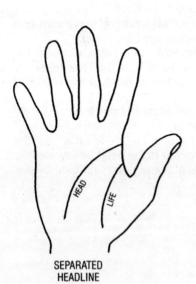

SEPARATED
HEADLINE

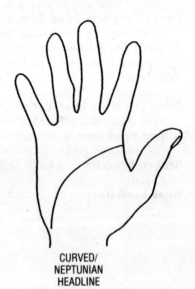

CURVED/
NEPTUNIAN
HEADLINE

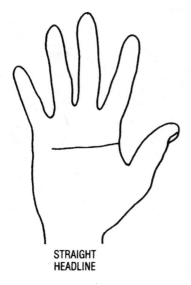

STRAIGHT
HEADLINE

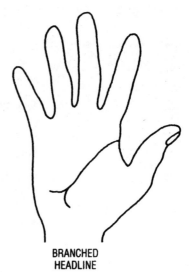

BRANCHED
HEADLINE

SPLIT
HEADLINE

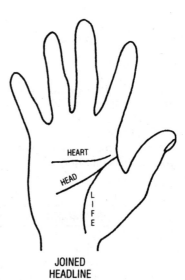

HEART

HEAD

L
I
F
E

JOINED
HEADLINE

Which type of hand do each of you have?

Person 1	Type	Person 2
_____	Standard	_____
_____	Separated	_____
_____	Short	_____
_____	Curved/Neptune	_____
_____	Straight	_____
_____	Split	_____
_____	Branched	_____
_____	Joined	_____
_____	Broken	_____
_____	Weak	_____

STANDARD STANDARD	4

The two of you share a healthy intellect. You greatly enjoy using your minds and have no patience for people with less developed mental faculties. Without a doubt, you'll keep each other intellectually stimulated. However, your relationship may lack a certain warmth because you can discuss ideas much better than you express emotion.

STANDARD SEPARATED	5

You're quite compatible. The separated-liner is a free-thinker who doesn't require much support from a partner. This works out well because the standard-lined individual doesn't want a clinging, dependent companion. You both can think for yourselves and fully respect each other's thoughts.

STANDARD	SHORT		1

You both need to be aware of the dissatisfaction that the other person may feel in the relationship—and then do whatever it takes to correct the situation. One of the major problems is that the short-liner may not feel that she or he is getting enough attention or affection from the standard-lined partner. This perception may actually be grounded in reality, since the standard-liner may tend to ignore the short-liner at times because she or he doesn't usually consider the short-lined partner to be an intellectual equal. A second concern is that while the standard-liner may initially enjoy the loving ministrations of a short-lined companion, later they may come across as cloying and suffocating. For your relationship to succeed, the standard-liner needs to show more respect and loving attention to the short-lined partner. The short-liner needs to be less overbearing in his or her affections and give the standard-liner some breathing space.

STANDARD	CURVED/NEPTUNE		4

For the most part, you'll get along well. The curved/Neptune-lined partner is more innovative than the standard-liner, but the standard-lined partner cherishes this in a companion. At times the curved/Neptune-lined individual may yearn for someone who more fully shares his or her creative talents, but in general the standard-liner provides a nice balance to the curved/Neptune-liner's life-style.

| STANDARD | STRAIGHT | 3 |

Yours won't be a very romantic or exciting relationship because you're both too sensible and practical to really let loose. But there won't be much friction in your life together. You share the same thoughts about most issues and can readily solve any problems through careful discussion. The standard-liner might sometimes wish that the straight-liner was more intellectually stimulating, but she or he will grow to respect the straight-liner's thoughtful consideration and judgment.

| STANDARD | SPLIT | 5 |

The split-lined individual will be a challenging partner for the standard-liner. There are many contradictory elements to the split-liner's nature, but the standard-lined partner should find this intriguing. At times the split-liner will appear to need to be independent; at other times she or he will want to lean on a strong partner. The split-liner will fluctuate between wanting a traditional life-style and one that is unconventional. Although the split-lined may always be an enigma to his or her partner, the standard-liner will enjoy trying to figure out what it is the split-liner really wants.

| STANDARD | BRANCHED | 5 |

You're ideally suited for each other. You both love to learn and to explore new ideas. You can't help but be knowledgeable and well-informed when you pool your intellectual talents. The standard-lined partner is no slouch in the brains department, but a branched-liner will definitely enhance his or her abilities. Moreover, the branched-liner brings an interest in other people that adds more human involvement to the standard-liner's tendency to be somewhat detached and aloof from other people (particularly those who don't share his or her intellectual prowess).

| STANDARD   JOINED | 1 |

The major challenge to your combination is that the joined-liner tends to perseverate too much on past ways of thinking. The joined-liner finds it difficult to break out of the mold she or he grew up in and can't shake traditional ideas and life-style even if they become obsolete. But the standard-liner needs a stimulating companion who is capable of growth and change. If the joined-liner wants to make the standard-lined partner happy, she or he must become more open to trying new things and taking risks. The standard-liner needs to be patient with the joined-lined partner and gently encourage him or her to experiment. It may take some time, but eventually you both can prosper in this relationship.

| STANDARD   BROKEN | 2 |

Life never runs smoothly when a broken-lined partner is in the picture. This unpredictability will ensure that things will never become dull, but it could cause some discomfort for the standard-liner, who never knows quite what to expect of the broken-liner. For your relationship to work, the standard-lined partner needs to develop optimal stress-management techniques to deal with the tensions that the broken-lined partner may cause. While it isn't in the broken-liner's nature to always think or behave in the same, routine way, he or she needs to be sure to let it be known that the one constant in his or her life is love for the standard-lined partner.

| STANDARD   WEAK | 2 |

If the standard-liner is very determined, she or he may be able to improve the intellectual abilities of the weak-lined partner. The weak-liner is not much interested in matters of a cognitive or spiritual nature, but the influence of a forceful standard-lined partner may begin to expose him or her to the pleasures of an active mind. However, if the standard-liner makes several unfruitful attempts to develop the weak-liner's intellect, there will be no point in continuing the relationship because you will have proven too different from each other to stay together in a harmonious fashion.

SEPARATED	SEPARATED	2

The two of you will have difficulty connecting with each other. Chances are that you both felt somewhat detached from your families as you were growing up and this alienation may be carried over into your present-day intimate relationships. You're each very individualistic, having your own unique thought patterns. This will lead to your talking *at* rather than with each other. But since neither one of you has any real desire for closeness, it shouldn't bother you that meaningful communication is so limited between the two of you.

SEPARATED	SHORT	1

You need to accept the fact that you're two very different people. Unlike the separated-line partner, the short-liner isn't interested in learning new things. Developing his or her intellect is not a priority for the short-lined partner, who is predominantly interested in making a happy home life and devotes all personal energies to this pursuit. Instead of trying to remake the short-lined partner into more of an intellectual, the separated-liner needs to respect and enjoy the short-liner's other abilities. The separated-liner should realize that she or he can engage in challenging debates and philosophical discussions with other friends but when wanting to be nurtured, the short-liner is a perfect partner.

SEPARATED	CURVED/NEPTUNE	4

You may not think exactly alike all the time, but your intellectual styles certainly mesh well together. You're both inclined to spend a great deal of time deep in thought. You value your cognitive capabilities and take pride in having a partner who is an intellectual equal. Your emotional needs, however, are not nearly as compatible as your thought processes. The separated-lined partner can be aloof and detached in a relationship, whereas the curved/Neptune-lined person attempts to ward off feelings of loneliness by pushing for an intense and close relationship. Luckily, the curved/Neptunian's creativity will allow him or her to find other emotional outlets to supplement whatever is missing in this relationship.

SEPARATED	STRAIGHT	3

You'll often find that you can't fully relate to how the other is thinking. The practical nature of the straight-lined partner is reflected in a sensible, straightforward cognitive mode. When there's a decision to be made, the straight-liner simply reviews the options and their consequences and then selects what appears to be the best alternative. Once the decision is made, the straight-liner never looks back while resolutely proceeding with the direction already chosen. But the separated-lined partner enjoys the process of mulling over a problem, considering a multitude of solutions, and continually reevaluating the efficacy of his or her choice. The straight-liner's style is too direct and concrete for the separated-line personality since it denies him or her the pleasure of all that contemplation. You'll never share the same intellectual style; but you can achieve mutual acceptance of your divergent styles.

| SEPARATED | SPLIT | 5 |

Both of you should be happy in this pairing. The intellectual separated-liner appreciates the stimulating duality of the split-lined partner. While other individuals may prefer a less challenging partner, the separated-liner revels in the unique paradox inherent in the split-lined personality: an attraction for the unusual accompanied by a need for the familiar and mundane, a desire to stand apart from the crowd concurrent with a need for universal acceptance. The considerable intellectual powers of the separated-lined partner enables him or her to ably assist the split-liner in fulfilling these conflicting needs and desires.

| SEPARATED | BRANCHED | 5 |

Neither of you could ask for a more suitable partner. You both are intrigued by a variety of ideas and thoughts. You love to be fully cognizant of everything that's happening in the world. Your mutual perceptivity to new ways of thinking will afford you unlimited experiences and challenges. Together you'll finely hone your intellectual skills to their greatest potential.

| SEPARATED | JOINED | 1 |

Understanding the other person does not come easily to either of you. The separated-lined partner finds it difficult to understand or respect the joined-liner's lack of intellectual integrity. The joined-line personality refuses to think for him- or herself. Instead, he or she has the mindset of his or her parents and is perfectly happy to think exactly as taught. The emotionally distant separated-liner has trouble relating to such close family ties as well as with accepting a partner who doesn't do his or her own thinking. Some changes are indicated on both your parts if you want a more fulfilling relationship. The joined-liner must become more independent, learning to formulate opinions and make decisions accordingly. The separated-liner needs to become more connected to family and friends for his or her own emotional growth as well as for the sake of the joined-lined partner.

SEPARATED	BROKEN	3

The broken-liner can either be a challenge or a burden to the separated-line partner. Only one thing is certain: the broken-liner will never bore the separated-liner. The stability of your relationship will depend on what happens with the broken-lined partner. If the broken-liner chooses to experiment with different ways of thinking and living, this won't upset the separated liner; to the contrary, the separated-line personality will find this fascinating. But if the broken-liner allows him- or herself to become weak intellectually and loses interest in trying to develop his or her mental processes, the separated-liner won't have the patience to deal with this situation. This couple's best hope for happiness is to avoid such a situation.

SEPARATED	WEAK	1

It takes some effort to effectively blend your two very different intellectual styles, but it's essential that you both try. If you don't compromise and learn to understand each other, the separated-line partner will bemoan the weak-liner's lack of interest in anything that's even remotely mentally challenging. The weak-liner will hold an equally derisive view of the separated-liner, seeing the highly intellectual separated-liner as insufferably pretentious and out of touch with reality. You need to improve your communication so that you each can gain a better perspective of what the other is all about. Honest and thorough discussions will eventually enable you to understand and accept your differences.

SHORT SHORT	5

Since neither one of you is interested in intellectual matters, there won't be much mental stimulation or growth in your relationship. But that's not a concern for a dual short-lined couple. You're both much more concerned with feelings than thoughts. Your hearts, not your heads, are what's important. Together you can find the warmth and love that is your primary goal in life.

SHORT CURVED/NEPTUNE	4

Intellectually, you don't have much in common. The curved/Neptune-lined partner is a highly creative thinker, whereas the short-liner isn't much interested in thoughts (particularly innovative or unique ones like those of the curved/Neptune-lined partner) and instead places his or her emphasis on feelings. Obviously, the curved/Neptune-lined individual will have to find intellectual companionship outside of the relationship to retain his or her active mental processes. But the two of you *can* connect on an emotional level. The curved/Neptune-lined partner may greatly enjoy a stimulating philosophical discussion but also wants the comfort of a loving partner. The short-lined partner is only too happy to provide this kind of unconditional love.

SHORT STRAIGHT	4

The straight-lined partner isn't overly intellectual, so it shouldn't be difficult for him or her to relate to a partner who shuns mental challenges in favor of affairs of the heart. While the short-liner is much more emotional than the careful and sensible straight-liner, a little passion can be just what the straight-lined person needs to really feel alive. When a decision has to be made, the straight-liner can be counted on to use good judgment and make the most appropriate choice. But the straight-liner doesn't have the ability to develop true intimacy in a relationship and this is where the short-liner has special expertise. Thus your differences can be quite complementary and, if used correctly, can result in a successful union.

SHORT	**SPLIT**	**2**

The good-hearted short-liner will try hard to accept a partner's idiosyncrasies, but may have difficulty with the conflicting and paradoxical nature of the split-liner. Just when the short-lined partner thinks she or he knows the split-liner, it will seem like the split-liner does a complete turnaround and becomes the opposite of what she or he previously appeared to be. While neither one of you can completely change your intrinsic natures, some attitude adjustment is both possible and essential. The split-liner needs to forewarn the short-lined partner before making any significant changes. This will ultimately reduce the stress levels for the short-liner since it prepares him or her for what will lie ahead. The short-liner, on the other hand, needs to view the split-liner's unpredictability in a more positive light. Rather than becoming upset about the lack of routine and structure, the short-lined partner can begin to appreciate the mystery and adventure associated with the split-liner.

SHORT	**BRANCHED**	**5**

If anyone can help the short-liner develop his or her intellectual capabilities, it is a branched-line partner. The open-minded versatility of the branched-liner enables him or her to relate to almost anyone, including a partner who is quite dissimilar. Because the branched-line personality is able to understand the short-liner's perspective and mode of thinking, she or he can gradually begin to expand the short-liner's mental faculties in a nonthreatening way. By emphasizing the emotional bond that's so important to the short-lined personality, the branched-liner can greatly encourage his or her partner to help your relationship prosper by maximizing both of your cognitive abilities.

SHORT	JOINED	5

The two of you are true soulmates. You both couldn't care less about intellectual accomplishments. Other people may devote extensive time and energy to improving their minds, but this pursuit doesn't have much appeal for you. You'd rather nurture the emotional side of your lives and develop a primary relationship that takes priority over everything else. Family is of utmost importance to both of you, so you'll be sure to surround yourselves with other people who bring additional love and support to your union.

SHORT	BROKEN	3

The broken-liner may not be the best partner in the world, but the short-liner doesn't care. Once a short-lined individual commits to someone, there's no turning back regardless of what happens. And because neither one of you devotes much thought to how you live, things will happen to you rather than your making them happen. This lack of control would be upsetting to some couples, but a short- and broken-lined pair avoids introspection and instead just copes with whatever arises. There might be a lot of trauma in your lives, but it won't tear you apart. The broken-lined partner is used to dealing with adversity and the short-lined partner will never give up on your relationship.

SHORT	WEAK	4

A short-lined individual is one of the few types who isn't upset by the weak-liner's lack of intellectual energy. The short-liner will totally accept his or her partner and will emphasize the positive aspects of the relationship rather than dwell on the negative. The two of you may not challenge each other's minds, but you can well offer love and support to your respective partners. As long as you're together, you can be happy with yourselves as individuals and as a couple. It doesn't matter that other people might be brighter, more sophisticated, or more successful than you because you're satisfied with what you've been given in life—namely each other.

| **CURVED/NEPTUNE** | **CURVED/NEPTUNE** | **5** |

Y our relationship is undoubtedly exciting. Both of you are highly creative thinkers who know how to keep things interesting. You each can come up with hundreds of ways to add a sense of mystery and adventure to your life together. While you understand and appreciate each other, your always-evolving personalities will prevent you from having to endure the stifling familiarity that's inherent in more static relationships. You'll each keep a fellow curved/Neptune-lined partner intrigued while allowing each other enough breathing space in your relationship so that you can pursue your individual needs and interests.

| **CURVED/NEPTUNE** | **STRAIGHT** | **1** |

B ecause the two of you think in totally opposite ways, there can be some difficulty at times relating to each other. The creative curved/Neptune-lined partner can't readily comprehend the straight-liner's somewhat inflexible mindset. Whereas the curved/Neptune-liner enjoys the challenge of experimenting with a variety of thinking and living styles, the straight-lined partner is most comfortable with the tried and true. Each of you needs to realize that there's something to be said for both your approaches. Combining them will ultimately enhance your lives as the straight-liner provides roots for stability and the curved/Neptunian adds wings to fly and reach your potentials. If you both keep an open mind about what the other can and does offer the relationship, you'll find that your differences can actually be advantageous.

CURVED/NEPTUNE   SPLIT   5

Your quick, active minds will do well together. You're both nonconformists who aren't afraid to differ from the established norm. You'll feel free to be true to your unique personalities with such compatible partners. Do whatever it takes to make your relationship work, because both of you would have difficulty finding another kindred spirit to share your lives.

CURVED/NEPTUNE   BRANCHED   5

Count yourselves among the fortunate few who are involved in such an ideal relationship. Your mutual open-mindedness and the excitement you share in learning will enable you to make your life together a never-ending adventure. You'll enjoy a wide variety of people and experiences that will take you in many directions. At times you'll go off on your separate ways to explore on your own, but inevitably you'll find yourselves being drawn back together. Both of you certainly have the brains to function independently of each other, but there's no sense in being alone when you each have a perfect companion in the other.

CURVED/NEPTUNE   JOINED   2

The differences in your thinking may be treasured at first by the curved/Neptune-lined partner, but she or he may become disenchanted as the novelty wears off and the reality of the joined-liner's rigid, unoriginal mindset becomes more and more apparent. For his or her own sake as well as that of the curved/Neptunian, the joined-liner must expand his or her intellectual horizons. Instead of simply adhering to the established way of doing things, the joined-liner must question whether alternative methods would be more beneficial. If the joined-liner becomes more receptive to breaking out of the usual routine, the curved/Neptunian will be much happier in the relationship (and the joined-liner may eventually discover that she or he enjoys learning and trying new things).

CURVED/NEPTUNE   BROKEN   **4**

The curved/Neptune-liner is a resourceful individual who can readily handle whatever turbulence the broken-lined partner brings into your shared life. Ups and downs are inevitable in anyone's life, but they're especially prevalent and dramatic when a broken-liner is involved. Fortunately, the curved/Neptune-liner enjoys challenges that allow him or her to use creative problem-solving. Occasionally, however, the curved/Neptune partner may become overly stressed by all the turmoil; when this happens, some "time out" from the relationship may be indicated. Even as brief a period as a weekend on his or her own will allow the curved/Neptune-lined partner to return to the relationship invigorated and refreshed.

CURVED/NEPTUNE   WEAK   **1**

Each of you needs to be considerate of the other person and try to put yourselves in his or her place. The curved/Neptune-lined partner must learn to be more sympathetic to the weak-lined partner's limited energy reserves. The relentless drive of the curved/Neptunian can be overwhelming for the less dynamic weak-liner. Gradual encouragement to partake more of life is preferable to exerting undue pressure on the weak-lined partner to suddenly change his or her ways. As for the weak-liner, he or she owes it to the curved/Neptunian to support his or her intellectual and creative activities. The weak-lined partner does not have to participate with the same enthusiasm or to the same degree as the curved/Neptunian, but the weak-liner should express interest in things that are important to the more dynamic partner.

| STRAIGHT | STRAIGHT | 5 |

You think exactly alike and consequently are extremely compatible. Disagreements will be a rare occurrence in your relationship because you share the same sensible, practical natures and will always see eye to eye with each other. Your life together will run smoothly because you both use sound, careful judgment at all times. You tend to stick with what you know, so there won't be many surprises or challenges in your lives. Other couples would be bored by this way of life, but the two of you are quite content and comfortable with your chosen life-style.

| STRAIGHT | SPLIT | 1 |

You both need to recognize the problems and issues in your relationship and then formulate strategies to resolve them. The straight-liner can be stressed by the split-liner's unconventional nature and fluctuating temperament. Conversely, the split-lined partner doesn't want to have to apologize for his or her eccentricities. Instead, he or she wants someone who will be tolerant of and even intrigued by his or her whims of the moment. But this is asking a lot of any partner and it's asking too much of a straight-lined partner. Most people (but especially the straight-liner) want at least some certainty and predictability in their lives. The split-lined partner must try to become a partner whom the straight-liner can depend on. While the straight-lined partner can never truly be sure exactly what the split-liner's thoughts and feelings will be at any given moment, she or he needs to feel that the split-liner's love is a constant. If the straight-liner can become a little more secure in the relationship and the split-liner tempers his or her moods even just slightly, you'll find more happiness together as a couple.

STRAIGHT BRANCHED	1

If you're not careful, the dissimilarities between your intellectual styles can cause you to constantly fight each other. The straight-liner may view the branched-lined partner as being unnecessarily and overly involved in the world of ideas, whereas the branched-liner can be unhappy with the straight-liner's limited intellectual approach.

Instead of criticizing the other person's way of thinking, learn to appreciate and take advantage of both your styles. When a quick decision needs to be made, use the straight-liner's no-nonsense approach. When a more complicated issue needs to be resolved, allow the branched-liner to contemplate the many different possibilities, both old and new. If you develop skill in merging your intellectual styles, you'll quickly discover that two heads truly are better than one.

STRAIGHT JOINED	4

No problems are anticipated with your combination. You take a similar approach in your styles of thinking and living. You're both happiest with what's familiar to you. In fact, neither of you (but especially the joined-liner) is likely to show much variance from your childhood personalities. You avoid change, viewing it as an unsettling phenomenon to be avoided at all costs. As a result, there probably won't be much intellectual or emotional growth in your individual selves or your relationship. But you're both satisfied with who you are and with each other, so there really isn't much need to make any modifications.

STRAIGHT BROKEN	2

When you first become involved with each other, the straight-lined partner will resolutely attempt to deal with the turbulence that the broken-liner brings into your lives. But after a while the straight-liner may feel that she or he has bitten off more than she or he can chew in this relationship. Typically, the only thing that the broken-lined partner can be depended on is to be undependable. Eventually, the clear-thinking straight-lined partner may become annoyed at the impetuous actions and poor judgment of the broken-liner. To avoid these negative feelings, the broken-lined partner needs to behave in a more rational and careful manner. Spontaneity is one thing, but running recklessly through life is something else. The broken-liner needs to emulate the example set by the straight-liner, letting this partner make many of the important decisions in your relationship.

STRAIGHT	WEAK	1

The two of you are basically compatible regarding your intellectual interests. You both place more emphasis on doing and being rather than thinking. But this doesn't mean that all will proceed smoothly in your relationship. Because the weak-liner is even less mentally energetic than the straight-liner, the weak-liner has the propensity to become too dependent on his or her straight-lined partner. It's unfair to the straight-liner if she or he is required to make all the decisions and shoulder all the responsibilities in your relationship. The weak-liner therefore needs to consciously push him- or herself to assume a more participative role in the relationship. The weak-liner must contribute to decision-making and problem-solving. The straight-liner must be firm about not allowing the weak-liner to shirk his or her responsibilities.

SPLIT	SPLIT	5

Never a dull moment with this combination! Your mercurial temperaments will make it impossible for you to take each other for granted. You'll never quite know how your respective partners will think or react in any situation. On one day, a split-liner will feel or need something that makes complete sense at the time; on the next day, she or he will do a complete turnaround and believe or want something entirely different. These inconsistencies would drive more stable personalities crazy, but you both can tolerate it because you share the same natures. The life of two split-liners won't be peaceful, but it will provide you with the ability to be true to yourselves without fear of what your respective partners will think.

SPLIT   BRANCHED   **5**

A split-branched pairing is certain to be compatible. Your mental wavelengths are very similar. You both are intrigued by a variety of ideas and enjoy experimenting with different life-styles. Together you'll challenge each other to function at your highest intellectual potentials. While you won't always agree with the choices that the other person makes, your mutual respect and open-mindedness will enable you to accept and deal with whatever the other feels is right at the time.

SPLIT   JOINED   **2**

Your intellectual styles are often dissimilar. The joined-liner has a very conservative personality that feels most comfortable with traditional ways of thinking and living. The split-liner may have moments where a tried-and-true approach seems best but can quickly grow restless with predictability and conventionality. When this occurs, the split-lined partner will abruptly embrace unique, contradictory, and even radical ideas and actions. For your relationship to work, the joined-liner has to learn not to be threatened by the split-liner's inconsistencies; they are simply an intrinsic part of the split-liner's intellectual makeup. The split-liner needs to accept rather than resent the joined-liner's insistence on order, routine, and familiarity. Mutual tolerance is essential for making your relationship viable.

SPLIT	BROKEN	1

You'll have a tumultuous life together. Both of you are given to extreme fluctuations in thoughts and emotions. Because you have such changeable natures, you'll never be quite sure where you stand with each other. Fortunately, you're both in a perpetual state of flux and neither one of you really expects a tranquil lifestyle. Other partners would be unnerved by all the changes you're continually involved in, but you each can accept this as a fact of life. Do be sure to learn some stress-management techniques so that you're best able to deal with the emotional and physical burdens caused by this never-ending series of ups and downs in your lives.

SPLIT	WEAK	3

Your combination is not ideal, but it can work because neither of you will place unrealistic demands on the other. A weak-lined individual won't offer much intellectual stimulation for the split-liner but is likely to be a sympathetic, nonjudgmental listener. The weak-liner will be a noncompetitive, supportive partner who will usually be tolerant of the split-liner's ever-changing whims and desires. When the split-lined partner experiences the need for someone who can provide more of a mental workout, she or he can draw upon a wide circle of friends.

BRANCHED	BRANCHED	5

Anything that either of you could want in a companion can be found in each other. You share the same thirst for intellectual stimulation and you both have the energy and determination to make your lives a nonstop learning experience. You'll never be bored as long as you're together; instead, you'll experience the heady rush of having partners who can ably assist in your intellectual and spiritual growth. There's no way that you'll always be going in the same direction, but this prospect intrigues (rather than threatens) you.

| BRANCHED   JOINED | 1 |

Since the branched-lined individual is receptive to a wide variety of ideas, she or he needs a partner who's equally open-minded. The joined-liner doesn't fit this need very regularly, but is quite inflexible and stubbornly clings to familiar thoughts and established ways of doing things.

If you want to improve your relationship, the branched-liner must become a sort of teacher and intellectual mentor who expands the joined-liner's horizons. The joined-liner needs to avoid stubbornly resisting attempts by the branched-liner to broaden his or her mind. Both of you will benefit from this strategy, the branched-liner by getting a more stimulating partner and the joined-liner by becoming more open and appreciative of new ideas and people.

| BRANCHED   BROKEN | 4 |

The branched-liner is extremely tolerant of his or her partner's idiosyncrasies and can cope successfully with the constant turmoil that comprises a broken-liner's life. There will be a great deal of instability in your relationship, but neither one of you favors consistency. You both prefer the challenge of developing and adapting new ways of thinking and living. The branched-line partner may occasionally need to temporarily retreat from the relationship if the broken-liner becomes too aimless or reckless, but in general you can relate well to each other.

BRANCHED	WEAK	1

The considerable mental prowess of the branched-liner cannot be matched by the weak-lined partner. The weak-liner just doesn't have the ability, energy, or know-how to provide complete intellectual satisfaction to the branched-lined partner. But this doesn't necessarily spell doom for your relationship. The branched-liner can receive intellectual stimulation from other sources (e.g., books, movies, classes, or challenging discussions with other people) while enjoying the emotional warmth brought by the weak-liner (and which wouldn't otherwise be present in a branched-liner's overintellectualized personality).

JOINED	JOINED	5

There's no question about your suitability to each other. You both care deeply about tradition, preferring to observe time-tested life patterns rather than experimenting with or inventing newer ones. Your shared conservative approaches are boring to more adventurous trendsetting types, but you're completely comfortable together. Don't let anyone put you down for your staid styles; it's one hundred percent right for you, and that's what counts.

JOINED	BROKEN	1

Yours can be a difficult pairing, particularly for the joined-lined individual. While the joined-liner's calm rationality may provide a welcome respite for the broken-liner on occasion, the broken-liner's disordered life-style can be very stressful for the joined-lined partner. This can prove to be disruptive and even destructive to your relationship. To avoid this potential problem, the joined-liner needs to zealously protect the serenity and predictability treasured in life. The joined-liner does not need to get involved in playing mind games with the broken-liner or in experiencing ideas and situations that will be uncomfortable. Instead, the joined-liner needs to reserve a special space in his or her life that is untouched by the broken-lined partner. The two of you can happily share a large part of your lives, but the joined-liner will always require that private space where she or he can find tranquillity.

	JOINED	WEAK		4

While this may not be a match made in heaven, it suits you both well and can last a lifetime. You'll have a static rather than dynamic relationship, but that's what you each prefer. The joined-lined partner won't be challenged by the weak-lined partner to do or to be anything other than what you two are naturally: quiet, unpretentious, unambitious. The two of you want nothing more than an undemanding life-style that doesn't place undue demands on your physical or intellectual energies. There is no doubt that you can find peace together and make each other happier than most partners ever could.

	BROKEN	BROKEN		3

A monotonous life-style is out of the question when two broken-liners are involved in a relationship. Since both of you experience a constant series of crises in your individual lives, your love life will be erratic, with extreme highs and lows. When things are good between you, you'll be challenged and excited by each other. But when the instability and tension escalates, you may find it difficult to be together. Learn how to soothe your individual and mutual stresses rather than add to them. Develop workable methods of dealing with the trying times of your lives.

| BROKEN   WEAK | 1 |

Hard work is required if you're both going to be happy in this relationship. The broken-liner needs a strong, capable partner who can cope with chaos. Unfortunately, the weak-liner doesn't typically have the intellectual fortitude for the extensive problem-solving required when a broken-liner is in the picture. But because the broken-liner can't easily change all the turbulence in his or her life, it falls to the weak-liner to improve his or her attitude and coping skills. Instead of resenting being called upon to exercise his or her mental faculties and viewing it as an additional burden, the weak-liner should see the need for analyzing problems and planning strategies as an opportunity for growth. This changed perspective on the part of the weak-lined partner will quickly result in both of you feeling more satisfied with each other and your life together.

| WEAK   WEAK | 4 |

Yours will be a lackluster pairing, but that won't bother either of you. The truth is that you prefer a relationship that is undemanding. You're not interested in taxing your intellectual abilities by trying to keep up with an energetic partner; you'd rather coast through life and exist on a comfortable plateau. You won't inspire each other to achieve your potential, but you'll be content with yourselves and your shared life.

Heart Line

The heart line reveals the romantic personality of an individual. Of the three major lines, this is the one that has the most significance for the emotional compatibility of an intimate relationship.

The standard heart line is clearly visible above the head line, beginning at the base of the index finger and running across the palm to end at the base of the little finger. Other variations of heart

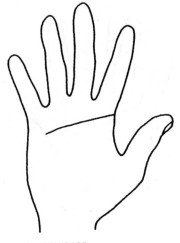

STANDARD
HEARTLINE

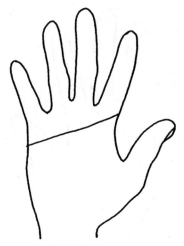

STRAIGHT
HEARTLINE

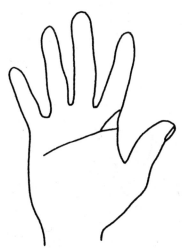

FORKED
HEARTLINE

JUPITER-SATURN
HEARTLINE

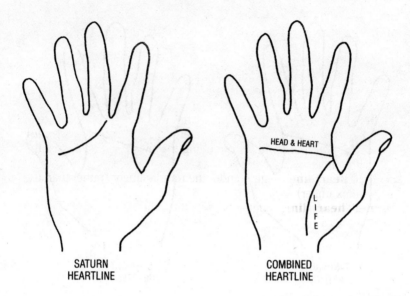

SATURN
HEARTLINE

COMBINED
HEARTLINE

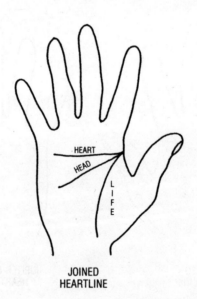

JOINED
HEARTLINE

lines are described below. Determine what type of heart line each of you has, then compare your types and read your romantic profile.

Forked heart line: begins with two or more lines under the base of the index finger and then merges into one main line

Straight heart line: begins on the extreme edge of the palm and travels a straight line to the other side

Jupiter-Saturn heart line: begins high up on the palm, between the index and middle fingers, then runs extremely close to the base of the other fingers, curving downward as it stops by the little finger

Saturn heart line: begins under the middle finger (rather than the index finger)

Joined heart line: connects with the other two lines (life and head) before they branch out on their own

Combined heart line: combines with the head line, giving the appearance of only two major lines rather than three

Person 1	type	Person 2
_____	Standard	_____
_____	Forked	_____
_____	Straight	_____
_____	Jupiter-Saturn	_____
_____	Saturn	_____
_____	Joined	_____
_____	Combined	_____

STANDARD   STANDARD   5

Your relationship can serve as the romantic prototype against which all other couplings can be compared. There will be no shortage of warmth and affection in your dealings with each other. Long-term stability will be just one of the many advantages of your union. You're both loyal and committed partners who can fully participate in the give-and-take of love.

| STANDARD | FORKED | 4 |

While there won't be major problems in your relationship, the forked-liner's emotional intensity can occasionally prove taxing for the standard-lined partner. Love is very important to the standard-liner, but it's an all-consuming obsession with the forked-liner. The forked-lined partner will go to extremes to please his or her partner, a trait that can be annoying to the standard-liner. If the forked-liner can learn to mellow a bit, the two of you should be quite happy together.

| STANDARD | STRAIGHT | 5 |

Standard- and straight-lined individuals are highly compatible and will enjoy a great deal of romance in their lives. You'll both give a great deal of yourselves to the relationship. The straight-liner does have a tendency to be blind to a partner's faults, but this doesn't matter in your situation since the standard-liner is an equally loving partner who would never take advantage of the straight-liner.

| STANDARD | JUPITER-SATURN | 4 |

The Jupiter-Saturn-lined individual is not the easiest person in the world to live with and love, but the standard-liner's emotional stability will enable this to be a successful union. Due to the Jupiter-Saturn liner's lack of self-confidence, she or he is easily jealous, but the standard-liner won't ever give him or her any reason to feel threatened or to doubt your relationship. The Jupiter-Saturn-liner also has difficulty expressing his or her feelings, but the standard-liner is secure enough not to require constant declarations of a partner's love and commitment.

| STANDARD   SATURN | 3 |

The standard-liner may be slightly dissatisfied with the Saturn-lined partner, but not to the extent that your relationship will be in jeopardy. At times, the standard-lined partner may wish that the Saturn-liner were more open and communicative. But fortunately the standard-liner has enough emotional resources of his or her own to tolerate a partner who is sometimes a little distant and aloof.

| STANDARD   JOINED | 2 |

You both need to work toward ensuring that your relationship survives over the long term. While the standard-liner won't readily give up on the two of you, she or he may reach a point of no return if the joined-liner becomes too emotionally dependent. The standard-liner doesn't mind occasionally letting a partner lean on him or her but needs to be firm about not allowing the joined-liner to become more of a burden than an equal partner. With encouragement the joined-liner can learn to stand on his or her own two feet. The joined-liner also must take care not to allow family problems to affect your relationship. He or she can still be close to his or her relatives, but they should not be permitted to interfere in your lives.

| STANDARD | COMBINED | 3 |

The combined-liner isn't the best partner for the standard-liner, but the two of you can nonetheless manage to have a very satisfactory relationship. The combined-liner is more comfortable relating to people on an intellectual rather than an emotional basis. The standard-lined partner needs to understand this and not have unrealistic expectations about receiving tangible expressions of affection from the combined-liner. Fortunately, the standard-liner is able to accept the combined-liner's undemonstrative manner because she or he is well-adjusted and secure enough to know that affection and commitment can be expressed in other ways besides the most obvious ones. To the standard-liner's credit, she or he realizes that the combined-lined partner is loyal and caring (even though he or she may have difficulty declaring his or her love in verbal, visual, or physical ways).

| FORKED | FORKED | 3 |

There won't be any shortage of affection in your relationship! You both are very outgoing, caring individuals who truly enjoy making other people happy. Each of you will go to great lengths to ensure that the other has everything she or he could possibly need or want. There's only one thing you may not be able to give each other: fidelity. Because you're both in love with love, you find it difficult being tied down to just one love object. If you're each willing to accept your respective partner's interest in other people, you'll have a blissful union. But if jealousy becomes a major factor, your relationship may not be able to survive.

| FORKED | STRAIGHT | 2 |

Both of you will totally throw yourselves into the relationship since you want more than anything else to have a richly rewarding romantic life. But problems are apt to occur when your expectations become too unrealistic. You're both likely to want more from a partner and a relationship than may actually be possible. As happy as you'll be when things are going smoothly, you'll be miserable when real life falls short of that romantic ideal. This may lead to your being unfaithful to each other as you attempt to find that perfect someone who can be your soulmate.

FORKED	JUPITER-SATURN	1

The Jupiter-Saturn-liner approaches love as carefully and seriously as everything else in life. This is in marked contrast to the forked-line personality, who deals with love in a more spontaneous and playful manner. Problems may mount if the Jupiter-Saturn-liner unhappily perceives the forked-liner's carefree attitude as a lack of caring. The Jupiter-Saturn-liner will be extremely distraught by the forked-liner's tendency to stray from your relationship. To make your relationship work, the forked-liner needs to understand that fidelity is very important to the Jupiter-Saturn-liner and refrain from doing anything that would violate that trust. But as long as the forked-liner is faithful, the Jupiter-Saturn should learn to appreciate his or her partner's lighthearted nature.

FORKED	SATURN	4

If you try hard to be sensitive to each other's needs, your relationship can work well even though you're so different from each other. The forked-liner has an exuberant, outgoing personality that complements the Saturn-liner's reserved nature. The Saturn-liner is more of a self-sufficient loner while the forked-liner wants a mutually interdependent relationship where you each could depend on the other for as much support as you need. It is essential that both of you respect your differences and try to develop strategies that offer a compromise between your individual personality traits.

| FORKED | JOINED | 2 |

Your relationship will have its share of problems. The joined-liner tends to be emotionally immature, but the forked-liner will usually be tolerant of a partner's shortcomings and accept him or her as a total package. At times, however, the joined-liner's total lack of self-reliance can prove suffocating as she or he looks to the forked-liner to make all the decisions and solve all the problems that affect you as individuals and as a couple. This can drive the forked-liner to stray outside the relationship to find a partner who functions as a person in his or her own right.

| FORKED | COMBINED | 3 |

The two of you are very different types of individuals. For your relationship to succeed, it is imperative that you accept who you each are. The combined-liner depends on his or her intellect to deal with the people in his or her life, whereas the forked-lined partner emphasizes the affective side. Thus the combined-liner tends to be reserved, even with his or her love partner; the forked-liner expresses his or her feelings openly and readily. It may be difficult at times for you to understand each other, but you both have enough energy (emotional and physical) to sort through your dissimilar styles and come to terms with them.

| STRAIGHT | STRAIGHT | 5 |

Each of you will be a constant source of delight for the other. You are both highly romantic and dedicate yourselves to making every day special. When things aren't going well for you, your mutual openness and excellent communication skills enable you to quickly work things out and get your relationship back on the right track. Other types of partners may feel that you're overly idealistic about love and expect more than can realistically be delivered, but you share the same desires and commitment for romance. You'll never disappoint each other; happiness is virtually guaranteed in a dual-straight-lined relationship.

STRAIGHT	JUPITER-SATURN	3

Love does not come as easily to a Jupiter-Saturn-liner as it does for a straight-liner. The Jupiter-Saturn-lined individual finds it difficult to express him- or herself. He or she would like to have a fulfilling love life but doesn't quite know how to make it happen. The Jupiter-Saturn liner lacks the self-confidence to take any romantic risks and will always opt to play it safe. She or he has trouble initiating displays of affection but can be a loyal and devoted partner. The straight-liner has a generous, giving nature and won't resent being the more openly expressive partner in the relationship.

STRAIGHT	SATURN	1

The basic difference between you is that the straight-liner wants a partner whom she or he can spoil and pamper, while the Saturn-liner is very self-sufficient and prefers to take care of things on his or her own. To resolve the potential problems that these opposing needs may cause, the straight-liner must develop a thicker skin and not view the Saturn-liner's independent nature as a personal affront. The Saturn-lined partner needs to realize that having the support of a loving partner like the straight-liner doesn't make him or her dependent or needy; it simply adds some warmth that would otherwise be missing in the Saturn-liner's life. If the Saturn-liner begins to accept the straight-liner's affections in a more gracious manner and the straight-liner learns to temper his or her time and energies so they don't become overwhelming to the Saturn-liner, the two of you can have a good partnership.

STRAIGHT	JOINED	3

It is not unusual for a straight-joined-lined pair to be together for a lifetime. The joined-lined partner is an emotionally needy individual who wants a partner to provide constant reassurance and tangible expressions of love. The straight-liner is only too happy to fulfill this desire since she or he needs to be needed. On the surface, your relationship will be an enviable one in which you both appear to be wrapped up in each other. In reality, things aren't quite as perfect as they appear. You tend to be too dependent on each other and neither of you could be considered emotionally mature. If a problem develops, you both are likely to fall apart (and possibly your relationship as well). Enjoy what you have together but be aware that life is not a fairy tale and remember that you both have some growing up to do.

STRAIGHT	COMBINED	1

You're two very different people emotionally. The combined-liner is not terribly interested in the sentimentality and romance that the straight-liner thrives on. Instead, the straight-liner prefers to conduct his or her love life in an efficient, businesslike way. As far as the combined-lined partner is concerned, it's enough that you're together; expressions of affection are nothing more than a waste of time. But being romantic is something that comes as naturally as breathing to the straight-liner. Therefore, the combined-liner needs to allow the straight-liner to express his or her feelings. Romantic gestures may be somewhat embarrassing to the combined-liner at times, but she or he must be gracious about accepting them from the straight-lined partner if your relationship is to succeed.

JUPITER-SATURN   JUPITER-SATURN   3

You're exactly alike, and this has both positive and negative implications for your relationship. Deep down you both are intense and passionate, but you don't know how to allow your true natures to be expressed. Instead, you tend to deny your feelings and limit your communication. You both want to be strong and in control, so you never take any risks. Neither of you would dream of allowing yourselves to be vulnerable in any way, so you go the opposite route and pretend to be more self-confident and independent than you really are. You're both capable of unfailing devotion to a partner, but you expect the same in return and easily become upset if you feel that the other isn't as committed.

JUPITER-SATURN   SATURN   4

There is little doubt that your relationship will last for a lifetime. You're very comfortable with each other because your love styles are so similar. You both have your share of insecurities, and this results in a mutual tendency to hold back. Neither of you could throw yourselves completely into a relationship; you prefer to proceed with caution. Even when you've been involved with a partner for some time, you still hesitate to fully express your feelings. You'll never communicate as well as other couples do, but that's okay with both of you . . . in fact, you prefer it that way.

JUPITER-SATURN   JOINED   1

It's crucial for you both to change your perspectives. Being overly critical of the other person will do nothing to enhance your relationship. If the Jupiter-Saturn-liner sees the joined-liner as being emotionally immature and overly dependent on his or her family, this lack of respect will prevent you from functioning as true equals. If the joined-liner feels pressured by the Jupiter-Saturn partner to become more independent, she or he may become extremely stressed and won't be able to function even semieffectively.

Avoid these negative consequences by each accepting the other for who she or he really is. The Jupiter-Saturn-lined partner can gently help the joined-liner gain more emotional strength but needs to realize that the joined-liner will never be the stronger partner. The joined-liner needs to make the most of the Jupiter-Saturn-liner's guidance and try to become his or her own person.

JUPITER-SATURN   COMBINED   **4**

This is a very workable combination. You both tend to hold back emotionally and prefer to relate to a partner in a more intellectual and formal manner. Displays of affection are seen by both of you as undesirable. The Jupiter-Saturn-liner limits his or her self-expression in an attempt not to appear weak or vulnerable; the combined-liner simply doesn't know any other way to function besides what has been so successful in his or her professional life. You'll be unwaveringly loyal to each other and will work hard to make your relationship last a lifetime. Other partners might be frustrated by what they would perceive as your coldness, but neither of you would feel comfortable leaving yourselves emotionally open. It works better for you both to have a committed but slightly detached relationship.

SATURN-SATURN   **2**

The two of you are very similar, but this doesn't always work to your mutual advantage. You're both reserved emotionally, so a lack of warmth and communication won't really bother either of you. However, there is the danger of you both being so self-sufficient that you don't allow any interdependency to develop. You each are so well able to function on your own that there often doesn't appear to be any reason for you to be together. Your feelings are easily hurt, yet both of you tend not to speak up and instead allow your unhappiness to grow rather than talking over any incidents in which one of you hurts the other. To decrease the possibility of growing apart, open communication is essential. You also need to emphasize shared projects and goals that involve the two of you together.

SATURN JOINED	1

Understanding each other's emotional styles presents a challenge to both of you. The joined-liner equates intimacy with dependency and clings to a partner for maximum support, whereas the Saturn-liner prefers to be self-reliant and for a partner to do the same. Be sure to talk and share your feelings so you can know where the other stands. Without adequate communication, the joined-liner may resent the Saturn-liner's aloofness and the Saturn-liner will feel suffocated by the joined-liner's never-ending emotional needs and demands. Learn to deal positively with the other person's temperament instead of allowing negative feelings to surface.

SATURN COMBINED	5

Neither of you is very demonstrative. You don't readily express affection. The fact that you're together is sufficient proof of your love; you don't need to show further proof of your commitment by verbal or physical means. This would be a liability if you were with other partners who needed frequent reassurance and affirmation. But with each other, you're completely comfortable and secure. You care deeply about each other, but neither of you wants to have to constantly worry about your respective partner's needs. Together you can conserve your energy for other important aspects of your lives (such as work).

| JOINED | JOINED | 2 |

You can easily be very dependent on each other, and this won't be at all healthy for either of you. Even though you're together as a couple, you must make sure you grow as individuals. If one of you is considering making any changes or reaching for a new goal, the other must encourage him or her in doing so. You also must be sure to cut the apron strings and not be excessively close to your families. Strive for mature love rather than just accepting a comfortable but limited relationship. Longevity is no problem in a double-lined pairing (you'll stay together longer than many combinations because you're at ease with each other and are too insecure to take the risk of switching partners), but you both need to expend some effort to reach your full potential as individuals and as a couple.

| JOINED | COMBINED | 5 |

This is a true complementary relationship, where each of you provides what is missing in the other. The combined-liner brings the intellectual element to the union. He or she is a thoughtful decision-maker who can use highly developed logical skills to plan your lives and solve any problems that arise. But the combined-lined partner's emotional development is typically very limited; he or she doesn't express or even acknowledge his or her feelings. The joined-liner is the perfect counterpart to the combined-liner, readily communicating warmth and affection. The joined-lined partner may not be as intellectual as the combined-liner but rescues the combined-liner from a life that would otherwise lack emotional warmth.

| COMBINED | COMBINED | 5 |

There won't be much intimacy in your relationship, but that's exactly how you both want it. You find emotions messy and therefore try to keep yours on hold. A calm, rational approach is your mutual style, both in business and in your love life. You prefer to intellectualize your feelings, dispassionately analyzing them and quickly moving past them to concentrate on things you find more comfortable and more important. Outsiders may not see much tangible evidence of your love, but the two of you are content with how you relate to each other. You obviously respect each other and are ideal helpmates in enabling your partners to set and reach high-level goals. Constant expressions of affection are something you both find superfluous; instead, you live your love on a daily basis by being supportive of each other's desires and ambitions.

Blood Type

Physicians have known for years that certain blood types make compatible donors for other blood types, but blood type compatibility has been taken a step further by a Japanese researcher. Toshitaka Nomi is convinced that specific personality traits are found in each of the four major blood types. Therefore, a couple with A and O types can be expected to have a different kind of a relationship from that of a B-AB pair.

Read on to learn more about your blood type combination. If you don't already know whether your type is A, B, AB, or O, a simple blood test performed at your doctor's office can determine which group you fall under.

Person 1	Type	Person 2
_____	A	_____
_____	B	_____
_____	AB	_____
_____	O	_____

	A A	2

Both of you are extreme perfectionists. You want every last detail to be exactly right and can't tolerate even minor imperfections. This characteristic can be quite beneficial in your jobs, but it causes a lot of friction in your relationship. There is a definite tendency to expect too much of yourselves and each other. When one of you fails to live up to these unrealistic expectations, the other typically feels betrayed and angry. Your inabilities to accept a partner's flaws and failings make a warm, loving relationship difficult (although not impossible).

Individuals with a blood type of A care deeply about their careers, often to the point of neglecting other, equally important aspects of their lives. After giving your all to work, neither of you may feel like expending the energy necessary to ensure a gratifying sexual or emotional relationship. Because this attitude can be very destructive to your relationship, you'll both need to push yourselves to devote sufficient time and energy to each other. Use some of that type A determination and diligence to maximize your relationship as well as your careers.

Both of you are highly susceptible to stress. Since stress can wreak havoc in your relationship (in addition to affecting your physical and emotional health), learn to relax together. Find a mutual activity or technique that diffuses stress (e.g., exercising, poetry, or painting) and pursue it together. Also try to let some things happen spontaneously in your lives rather than planning everything out. Most important, learn to become more tolerant of each other's shortcomings. Don't expect your partner or yourself to be perfect; strive instead for the more obtainable goal of being the best you can be.

	A B	5

The two of you don't share any major personality traits. In fact, you are mirror opposites of each other. Whereas the A individual is conservative and restrained, the B is free-spirited and imaginative. The B partner has an almost childlike quality as compared to the more mature A. Your philosophies of life are entirely different. B lives for the moment while A carefully considers the future implications of any action. B lets loose with his or her emotions; A keeps a tight check on them.

Can a relationship between two such different people succeed? The good news is that an A-B pairing can be fulfilling for both partners. Each of you can offer something quite special to the relationship. The B partner can help the A to loosen up and take some risks, thus enabling him or her to enjoy life more fully. B is the ideal partner to expose A to the magic of art, music, and literature. On the other hand, the A can provide a stabilizing influence for the rash and often reckless B. Since the B has a tendency to act without thinking, the A's thoughtful approach to everything in life is a much-needed counterbalance to the B's impulsivity and can keep him or her out of trouble. And although B types can be highly emotional, they tend to fight less with A partners than with any other blood type.

You have the potential for a terrific relationship. Just be sure to keep an open mind regarding each other's personality traits. You each have qualities the other doesn't. Recognize and accept that fact; don't make the mistake of trying to change him or her in your image. Instead of being jealous of the other person's strengths, cherish them and use them. By retaining your two distinct personalities, your partnership will remain a growing experience.

A	AB		4

Couples with these two blood types generally don't have any major problems. Since the A and AB types are both pragmatic and determined, the two of you will do whatever it takes to make the relationship work. You're not like other couples, who give up at the first sign of trouble; you're willing to work through your difficulties until they're resolved. This high degree of commitment ensures a long-lasting, stable relationship.

Although you're well suited to each other in most respects, there are some inherent differences between your types. The AB has more of a tendency to be moody than the A, who usually remains on a fairly even keel. Even in extremely trying circumstances, the A keeps a tight rein on his or her emotions and holds stress in rather than expressing it. The AB, on the other hand, seldom internalizes stress and instead manifests it through changes in behavior patterns. Whereas the A can always be counted on to behave in a predictable manner, there can be dramatic fluctuations in an AB's personality and actions. This can be more than a little discomfiting for the A partner.

Unfortunately, it's not realistic to expect an AB (no matter how hard he or she tries) to maintain a calm, steady temperament. The A partner has to learn to cope with the AB's ups and downs. Rather than bemoaning the AB's lack of stability, the A should enjoy the surprises that prevent the relationship from ever getting into a rut.

Another difference is that the AB partner is more people-oriented than the A. The AB is highly social while the A is somewhat of a loner. It is essential for the A to have some time alone, but the gregarious AB may find it difficult to understand this need. Some friction could occur if the AB mistakes the A's restraint for a lack of caring. It is crucial for the AB to recognize that an A is not demonstrative by nature and doesn't openly express affection. However, once an AB really gets to know an A, she or he will discover a deeply loving, intensely loyal partner. With a little bit of nurturing from both partners, the A-AB relationship can flourish for a lifetime.

| A   O | 2 |

Yours is a difficult partnership. You're both high-strung, but your emotions and energy are not always channeled in appropriate ways. There is apt to be a great deal of fighting between the two of you since control is a big issue. The O partner is quite assertive, sometimes to the point of being aggressive, and craves power in romantic as well as business relationships. The A partner is more of a pacifist and may sometimes want a more dominant role in the partnership. A power play can develop; when this occurs, it is likely that both of you will lose. Bitterness, resentment, and hostility may cloud your positive emotions for each other. Therefore, it is important for you to try to work toward an egalitarian relationship where neither of you is boss. If you can function as equals, you both will feel more secure and satisfied.

Both A and O individuals are sticklers for detail and strive for perfection in every aspect of their lives. However, the A frequently carries this trait to an extreme. Because perfection is such an unobtainable goal, the A tends to be the less satisfied partner and may dwell on the parts of the relationship that are less than ideal while overlooking the positive elements. Fortunately, the O is more realistic and can better accept flaws in a partner and a relationship. It falls upon the O to keep things in the right perspective and to remind the A about what drew you together in the first place. This will help the A to realize that even though things aren't perfect, your relationship is still worthwhile.

A and O individuals differ in the way they feel about themselves. O's have a great deal of self-confidence. They know exactly who they are and are comfortable with that knowledge. Consequently, they're not especially concerned about what other people think of them. A's, on the other hand, have less intrinsic confidence and care deeply about how others perceive them. The A can't feel secure in a relationship without constant reassurance and affirmation of his or her desirability. The O needs to oblige this need by being as loving and supportive as possible. Once the A feels truly loved, she or he will reciprocate the affection and become an excellent partner for the O.

B	B		3

You both are true individualists with your own unique styles. Unlike other couples who share the same blood types, you're quite different from each other. Nonetheless, there are some basic traits you share in common. Both of you need a lot of freedom in your relationship. You need room to breathe, space to grow. Both being B's, each understands the other's desire for independence, whereas other blood types might smother or overwhelm you with their attempts to control you or to make excessive demands.

Another shared characteristic is your assertive natures. Each of you stands up for what you believe in; neither one is afraid to fight for what you know is right. As a result, it's impossible for either of you to take advantage of the other. Your relationship is firmly grounded in equality. There isn't the type of inequity seen in relationships where one partner is extremely aggressive and the other quite passive. However, there can be a great deal of competition between you. This competitive element can have quite positive results since it inspires both of you toward enhanced creativity. In your striving to keep up with and surpass each other, you'll find that your personal potential reaches new heights that you wouldn't have thought possible.

The downside of a B-B pairing is that you tend not to function as a couple; you're more likely to live as two completely separate individuals who only occasionally come together to form a union. Therefore, it's important for you to set aside as much time as possible to pursue activities of mutual interest. Since you're both active people who are always on the go, be sure to also designate some quiet time together where you can talk about your dreams and plans. Try to be fully involved in your partner's life and not just in your own. Read books and attend workshops on becoming more supportive and caring partners. Always keep in mind that although each of your lives is fulfilling in its own right, everything becomes even better when you can share it fully with someone you truly love.

B AB	3

B-AB relationships usually won't have insurmountable problems if each of you tries to understand and accept the differences between you. For example, the AB partner will tend to want to spend as much time together as possible while the B needs some private time. Obviously the only solution is to compromise. The B individual, if she or he truly wants the relationship to work, has to be willing to give up some solitary time and devote more attention to the AB partner. The AB has to come to terms with the B's independence and develop more of his or her own self-reliance.

It takes a special person to accept the B's individualism. The B is a true nonconformist who makes his or her own way in life. Anyone who is involved with a B has to be prepared to cope with a life that is unpredictable and even unstable at times. There isn't much of a comfort zone for the non-B partner, who never knows entirely what to expect from the B. Fortunately, the AB is a fairly tolerant partner who respects the B's innovative nature and creativity. In most instances, the AB will be quite supportive of the B's "marching to the beat of a different drummer." This is not to imply, however, that the B can expect unconditional acceptance at all times. The AB does have his or her limits. Most AB's experience frequent episodes of moodiness. In an up phase, the AB will be delighted by almost anything the B does. But when down, the AB can bitterly resent the B for making life complicated and difficult. During these times, the B needs to tone down his or her intensity and try harder to accommodate the AB's wants and needs. If you each can meet the other halfway, you'll dramatically enhance the happiness of your relationship as well as promote growth in your individual selves.

B O	2

Because each of you has such a strong personality, frequent clashes of wills are inevitable. You want different things from your relationship and you're both determined to get them. Unfortunately, neither of you is good at compromise. The O partner is used to getting his or her own way, having established a lifelong pattern of winning in most interpersonal situations. The B isn't concerned about power for its own sake but does need a sense of autonomy. It is impossible for the B to live by someone else's standards. If your relationship is to survive, each of you will have to develop more tolerance for the other's ideas and actions. You'll need to recognize—and accept—that you can't change your partner into a clone of yourself. Look at your differences as something that makes life interesting rather than as an obstacle to overcome. When you need to come to a mutual consensus about an issue, be sure to negotiate in a way that ensures both of you can win.

Although B and O types are both active, dynamic personalities, there are some inherent dissimilarities. The O is very detail-oriented, whereas the B is able to see the more global picture. Consequently, the O partner may tend to focus on aspects of the relationship that are negative but relatively minor. This can cloud the O's perspective to the point where she or he can't ever see anything positive about the relationship. It is up to the B to remind the O about your *total* relationship. The positive aspects need to be capitalized upon while working toward solutions to the problems that interfere with your mutual happiness.

Another difference between the two of you is the way each approaches new things. Once an O becomes comfortable with someone or something, she or he is likely to reject change of any kind. The O is perfectly happy with leaving things exactly as they are and not experimenting with any innovations. The B, on the other hand, thrives on change and has trouble coping when things become too predictable. Therefore, the B is more apt to find the relationship boring and stagnant than is the O. This fact needs to be dealt with in a constructive way. The B needs to learn to appreciate the stability that the O provides; without this constancy, the B might compulsively seek constant change and stimulation to the point where his or her life would lack any focus. The O needs to become more receptive to trying new things. Thus each partner can provide an important dimension that would otherwise be missing in the other person's life.

AB   AB   **1**

With two AB partners, your relationship is sure to be a rocky one. Both your natures are highly changeable, with tempers that flare easily and emotions that can be precariously unstable. Needless to say, this can result in frequent arguments. It is fair to note that AB-AB couples fight more often and more intensely than any other pairing. This can eventually result in the destruction of the relationship.

If the two of you want your relationship to last, you'll need to develop some strategies for dealing with your mutual emotional volatility. Limit the amount of time you spend together. While it is natural for you to enjoy each other's company, you may actually find that your appreciation of your partner increases if you spend some time apart. Learn to recognize and heed the warning signals that let you know things are getting too intense. A little distance can improve your perspectives and refresh both of you so that you can devote full energy to enhancing your relationship.

AB's are very pragmatic people. You focus on the essentials and avoid the more trivial or nebulous details that detract from the overall picture. This single-minded, straightforward approach enables you to reach the goals you set for yourselves in most areas of your lives, but it may be less beneficial in terms of romance. Making well-defined plans is necessary at work, but you need to be more flexible and spontaneous in your relationship. Take advantage of serendipitous events; do things on the spur of the moment. And don't neglect the little things which, although they may not seem overly important on the surface, can add to your enjoyment of being a couple. Establish rituals and traditions that bind you together; give each other small gifts on a frequent, no-occasion, "just because" basis; maintain a sense of humor and playfulness in everything you do.

AB O	**3**

It's crucial for you to establish mutual goals to work toward together since it would be detrimental for you to compete against each other. Other couples may be able to engage in friendly competition on the tennis courts or even in the work world, but this is not appropriate for an AB-O pair. The highly competitive O, determined to win regardless of the cost, can become ruthless and hurtful in his or her striving to be number one. Obviously, this is not in the AB's best interests. The AB can't really compete with the O's relentless determination; it wouldn't be a fair contest. The self-esteem of the AB can be destroyed if she or he begins to feel like a failure in comparison to the O. Therefore, any sort of competition should be avoided. Be sure to work *with,* not against, each other. If you don't already have them, develop interests and goals both of you can be comfortable with and help each other enjoy them.

An AB-O relationship does have some positive elements. The AB is much more open and emotional than the O. The AB can encourage the O to learn to be more expressive and loving, thus adding another dimension to the O's personality. The O, on the other hand, can help the AB set high standards for his or her own achievement. Because the O expects a great deal from a partner, the AB will try to measure up to this standard. Thus, the AB (who if left to his or her own devices might tend not to push toward self-development) will have a role model and mentor who does strive to reach his or her personal potential.

O   O | 1

W hen two O's are romantically involved, there is bound to be a struggle for power. Each of you wants to be in the forefront at all times, calling the shots and making the decisions. Both want to be leaders; it's completely foreign to your natures to passively follow someone else's lead. This can be quite a problem since it's often impossible for you both to be in control at the same time. Unless you have unlimited resources of time, energy, and money, there will be occasions when choices and tradeoffs have to be made. It's very probable that both partners' needs and desires won't be equally satisfied in every instance. A more easygoing type might be able to accept this fact, but an O has great difficulty with any sort of occurrence that could be perceived as a loss. Even if the "loser" didn't care all that strongly about the particular issue in question (e.g., something as relatively trivial as where to go out to eat or what movie to see), it's still taken as a personal affront when his or her wishes aren't granted. Resentment or anger typically follows, two emotions that are destructive for a loving relationship.

If you're convinced that there is enough that's good in your relationship to warrant the effort needed to sustain it, you'll need to devise a game plan for dealing with the inescapable conflicts that arise. Don't wait until your next heated argument to try to make a decision; instead, discuss the overall problem when you're both calm and rational. Neither of you should have difficulty recognizing the obvious inability for both to be in charge at the same time in every situation. A workable solution could be to designate who will make what decisions and when. Each partner may have expertise in certain areas; it makes sense for that person to take control of that area. Or you can decide to be completely democratic and take turns making the decisions (e.g., each choosing the activities on alternate weekends). Professional counseling can also be helpful.

In terms of the outward manifestations of success, a double-O couple is the pair most likely to appear to have it all. But this can be just an illusion. An O often feels that something indefinable but important is lacking in his or her life regardless of the amount of personal wealth. It is possible that the missing ingredient is the ability to connect with someone else on more than a basic level. It may not be easy for an O to become vulnerable to the point where she or her can deeply relate to another human being. It certainly isn't easy for two O's to develop this ability with each other. But it *can* be done and it's worth the hard work. Once you truly are able to enjoy an emotionally intimate and caring relationship, you'll find that you really do have it all!

TOTAL COMPATIBILITY PROFILES

If you take all the tests in the book and add up your scores, your total score can range from a low of 15 to a high of 100. Your total compatibility score indicates a general compatibility or incompatibility between the two of you, as described below.

86–100

COULDN'T BE BETTER

No doubt about it . . . you truly are perfect partners! In every way that counts, you're very much alike. In some instances, you may have slightly different personality traits, but these complement (rather than clash with) each other. Because you share the same desires and goals, you'll work extremely well together in developing the type of life-style you both want. There's very little that you need to do to keep your relationship special. Just be sure to count your blessings that you each found your ideal partner.

71–85

LOOKING GOOD

The two of you are well suited to each other. You're not identical in terms of temperament or character traits, but you still have plenty in common. However, it's important that you don't become too complacent. As good as your relationship is now, there is still the possibility of your growing apart if you don't make a conscious effort to respect, appreciate, and communicate with each other.

56–70

NOT BAD AT ALL

Compatibility between you is average. But don't despair; this doesn't necessarily forewarn trouble in your relationship. You'll have your ups and downs, but you'll still be glad (almost all the time) that you're together. Like most couples, there will be misunderstandings and disagreements from time to time. If you're committed to each other, however, you can learn from these occasions and make your relationship stronger than ever.

41–55

WORTH THE EFFORT

While you're far from an ideal couple, you can still find reasons to stay together. There will undoubtedly be a good deal of friction between you because you often find it difficult to understand each other. But the bright spots of your relationship make up for the rough times. Be sure to set some time aside on a regular basis to look at what's good about your relationship instead of just focusing on the all-too-obvious problems.

26–40

DANGER ZONE

Your coupling won't last unless you both devote yourselves to constant monitoring of your relationship. You have precious little in common; instead, you see almost everything from totally different perspectives. Fights will be frequent and you'll often be tempted to split up. But your relationship *can* work if you attend to problems as soon as they develop, possibly even seeking help from outside sources when you can't resolve certain issues on your own.

15–25

LOST CAUSE

Your low score probably isn't a big surprise to either of you. You've probably both suspected that there really isn't much point to your being together. While there may have been some sort of initial attraction, you may later discover that you're too different to get along with each other. Cut your losses before you invest any more time in this no-win relationship and find more compatible partners.

SCORE SHEET

Brain dominance . . . . □

Birth order . . . . □

Handwriting . . . . □

Humor appreciation . . . . □

Color preference . . . . □

Sleep position . . . . □

Exercise preference . . . . □

Pets . . . . □

Decorating style . . . . □

Food preference . . . . □

Birth experience . . . . □

Body type . . . . □

Eye Color . . . . □

Hands ($\underset{\text{life}}{_____}$ + $\underset{\text{head}}{_____}$ + $\underset{\text{heart}}{_____}$) ÷ 3 . . . . □

Blood type . . . . □

TOTAL . . . . □

SCORE SHEET

Brain dominance .... □

Birth order .... □

Handwriting .... □

Humor appreciation .... □

Color preference .... □

Sleep position .... □

Exercise preference .... □

Pets .... □

Decorating style .... □

Food preference .... □

Birth experience .... □

Body type .... □

Eye Color .... □

Hands (_____ + _____ + _____) ÷ 3 .... □
        life   head   heart

Blood type .... □

TOTAL .... □

SCORE SHEET

Brain dominance . . . . □

Birth order . . . . □

Handwriting . . . . □

Humor appreciation . . . . □

Color preference . . . . □

Sleep position . . . . □

Exercise preference . . . . □

Pets . . . . □

Decorating style . . . . □

Food preference . . . . □

Birth experience . . . . □

Body type . . . . □

Eye Color . . . . □

Hands (_____ + _____ + _____) ÷ 3 . . . . □
       life   head   heart

Blood type . . . . □

TOTAL . . . . □

ABOUT THE AUTHOR

ELLEN LEDERMAN has been interested for many years in psychology and alternative systems for understanding personality and character traits. Extensive study and research have led her to the conclusion that there are many varied methods for interpreting human behavior and emotions. Rather than specializing in just one body of knowledge (such as astrology, numerology, or graphology), she prefers to use an eclectic approach that embraces a wide variety of ancient and modern theories. Working closely with people as a therapist and counselor has enabled her to test these concepts and to develop new insights about how different types of people relate to one another. She is pleased to report that she is married to her perfect partner: a left-brained, green-eyed vegetarian who swims, favors the color blue, sleeps in a semifetal position, and has a blood type of O.